Twenty-First-Century
SOUTHERN
WRITERS

Twenty-First-Century
SOUTHERN
WRITERS

•

New Voices, New Perspectives

Edited by Jean W. Cash and Richard Gaughran

University Press of Mississippi / Jackson

The University Press of Mississippi is the scholarly publishing agency of
the Mississippi Institutions of Higher Learning: Alcorn State University,
Delta State University, Jackson State University, Mississippi State University,
Mississippi University for Women, Mississippi Valley State University,
University of Mississippi, and University of Southern Mississippi.

www.upress.state.ms.us

The University Press of Mississippi is a member
of the Association of University Presses.

First printing 2021
∞

Library of Congress Cataloging-in-Publication Data

Names: Cash, Jean W., 1938– editor. | Gaughran, Richard, 1952– editor.
Title: Twenty-first-century southern writers : new voices, new perspectives
/ Jean W. Cash, Richard Gaughran.
Description: Jackson : University Press of Mississippi, 2021. | Includes
bibliographical references and index.
Identifiers: LCCN 2020054691 (print) | LCCN 2020054692 (ebook) | ISBN
9781496833334 (hardback) | ISBN 9781496833341 (trade paperback) | ISBN
9781496833358 (epub) | ISBN 9781496833365 (epub) | ISBN 9781496833372
(pdf) | ISBN 9781496833389 (pdf)
Subjects: LCSH: American literature—Southern States—History and
criticism. | American literature—Southern States—21st century.
Classification: LCC PS261 .T94 2021 (print) | LCC PS261 (ebook) | DDC
810.9/975—dc23
LC record available at https://lccn.loc.gov/2020054691
LC ebook record available at https://lccn.loc.gov/2020054692

British Library Cataloging-in-Publication Data available

Contents

Introduction

Readers who know and appreciate literature of the American South from the past one hundred years are aware that William Faulkner was pivotal in creating what Louis Rubin termed a "southern literary renaissance." Though writers have disputed the validity of the designation, it's clear that the success of Faulkner as a writer of both the Old and the New South helped stimulate other writers from the region to expand on his legacy. Writers who followed him used their particular areas in the South, as he did, to deal with universal themes like loneliness and alienation, race, and the depletion of the South's natural resources.

His immediate followers, particularly Eudora Welty, Flannery O'Connor, Walker Percy, William Styron, and Ralph Ellison, flourished in Faulkner's wake. In works like *The Gold Apples*, Welty, who long wrote in Faulkner's shadow, dealt with issues of love, family, and race in an updated South. Drawing on her native Georgia in her short stories and novels, O'Connor emphasized the need for genuine Christian faith in an increasingly unbelieving world; from Louisiana, Percy, too, in novels like *The Moviegoer*, was concerned with finding a link to a God who seemed nearly inaccessible in the malaise of the modern world; Styron had personally given up on Christianity, filling the void with a reliance on artistic creation. In the process of a varied career, however, using his native Virginia as setting, Styron produced one of the most important twentieth-century fictional studies of race when he wrote *The Confessions of Nat Turner* at the height of the civil rights movement. The novel helped stimulate debate, and controversy, that continues to the present. With *Invisible Man*, Ellison, from Oklahoma, created a fictional masterwork concerned with race and identity.

The success of these writers during the second half of the twentieth century helped encourage many others to present their views of the southern experience. Some of these writers, like Lee Smith, Clyde Edgerton, and Ron Rash, celebrated southerners' resilience while lamenting the end of the agrarian South and the increasing industrialism that ruined its natural beauties. During the last twenty years of the century, the most interesting new development was the rise of writers from working-class backgrounds, who, for the first time, told what it was really like to live in a rural South without the benefit of education and financial security. The progenitor of this group was Harry Crews from Georgia, whose most significant novel, *A Feast of Snakes*, tapped into the hopelessness of people—white and Black—struggling to transcend the poverty and depravity into which they were born. Crews motivated writers like Tim McLaurin, Dorothy Allison, Larry Brown, William Gay, and Tom Franklin to write novels that provide a variety of ways to survive in hostile environments.

Writers during the first twenty years of the current century caught us by surprise with their number, diversity, and talent. Discovering and reading novels by this group of writers who began their careers after 2000 stimulated us to collect and organize the essays that appear in this volume. We have included essays about nineteen of these writers, at the same time acknowledging that there are others, equally talented, whom we have missed.

These writers' works cover wide-ranging subjects and themes: the history of the region, the continued problems of the working-class South, the racial divisions that have continued, the violence of the modern world, and the difficulties of establishing a spiritual identity in a modern context. The approaches and styles vary from writer to writer, with realistic, place-centered description as the foundation of many of their works; they have also created new perspectives regarding point of view, and some have moved toward the inclusion of magic realism in their work.

Some of the nineteen whom we have covered follow in the tradition of the Rough South writers mentioned earlier: Michael Farris Smith, Brian Panowich, Steph Post, Taylor Brown, David Armand, Joe Samuel Starnes, Skip Horack, David Joy, and Lee Clay Johnson. At the same time, these writers have combined other elements with their treatment of underclass characters. Michael Farris Smith sees personal identity as central to his characters. Brian

Panowich in *Bull Mountain* is much concerned with the influence of drug culture on the rural South; he also emphasizes the importance of "outlaw" country music in the lives of his characters. Steph Post emphasizes major changes in the Florida landscape. Taylor Brown has incorporated elements of Georgia history into some of his fiction. Many of the writers, such as Barb Johnson, write coming-of-age tales in a southern context or, like Wiley Cash, develop characters searching for redemption for past transgressions. David Armand concerns himself with particular problems of identity in the modern South, and Lee Clay Johnson in *Nitro Mountain* includes bluegrass music as an accompaniment to the action.

Several of the writers have produced what we presume to call "novels of manners" in the contemporary South. Inman Majors deals with middle-class characters striving to find meaning in the contemporary South. His major novel *The Millionaires* clearly demonstrates how money and power have become corrupting influences in parts of the South. Stephanie Powell Watts deals with the lives of middle-class African Americans in her novel *No One Is Coming to Save Us* and, like Majors, shows the ruinous effects of money. In her four novels to date, Tayari Jones deals primarily with family issues and the quest for individual identity; her novel *An American Marriage* deals both with the way racism persists within the southern system of justice and with problems of money and marriage on a smaller, domestic scale. In her first novel, *Leaving Atlanta*, Jones employs multiple first-person narrators in reliving the series of child murders that occurred in Atlanta in the 1980s. Similarly drawing on headlines from the recent past, Ravi Howard, in *Like Trees Walking*, uses a modern incident of lynching in Mobile, Alabama, as the genesis of his novel.

Jesmyn Ward also fictionalizes recent events, drawing on her own experience to write arguably the greatest novel to emerge in the wake of Hurricane Katrina, her award-winning *Salvage the Bones*. Also a Mississippian, Ward doesn't disguise the Faulkner influences, consistently setting her fiction in an invented place, Bois Sauvage, recalling Faulkner's Yoknapatawpha County. Furthermore, *Salvage the Bones* in some ways revises Faulkner's *As I Lay Dying*; and her second National Book Award winner, *Sing, Unburied, Sing*, employs Faulknerian multiple narratives combined with elements of magic realism.

Jamie Quatro, Thomas Pierce, and Karen Russell have written novels that—in the vein of O'Connor—deal with achieving spiritual identity in a modern South. In a review of O'Connor's *A Prayer Journal* in *Oxford American*, Quatro writes of the conflict between the erotic and the spiritual evidenced in O'Connor's early diary. The same intersection and conflict between sexual desire and spiritual faith permeate Quatro's own fiction, particularly in her recent novel *Fire Sermon*. Thomas Pierce is much concerned with questions of ultimate reality, in this world and what lies beyond. Though firmly grounded in place, Karen Russell, too, is concerned with what lies beyond our material existence.

The works of southern writers who have begun their careers since the year 2000 are noteworthy for their variety, demonstrating the influence of the past, but also the need for new perspectives. The critical essays in this volume place these emerging artists in the context of southern writers from the past, but they also demonstrate the ways in which these artists have experimented, both renewing and reworking what has come before, promising that southern literature will continue to express itself with a distinctive voice, one that will speak with authority in the decades to come.

Jean W. Cash
Richard Gaughran

Twenty-First-Century
SOUTHERN WRITERS

Barb Johnson grew up in semirural Lake Charles, Louisiana, surrounded by rice fields and natural gas refineries. In 2004, after more than twenty years of working as a carpenter in New Orleans, she entered an MFA program at the University of New Orleans. The next year, however, Hurricane Katrina hit the city, destroyed Johnson's carpentry shop, and forced her to evacuate. Using a fake Centers for Disease Control ID, Johnson sneaked back into New Orleans and started writing what would become her first published collection of short stories, *More of This World or Maybe Another*. Since the collection's publication in 2009, Johnson has continued to write and publish short stories. She also contributed an autobiographical essay to Sonny Brewer's *Don't Quit Your Day Job: Acclaimed Authors and the Day Jobs They Quit*. Johnson recently finished writing her first novel, which revolves around the characters introduced in *More of This World or Maybe Another*. It takes place after the climax of the collection's final story.

The "Sweet Dark Heart" of Louisiana
Individual Authenticity and Barb Johnson's
Working-Class New Orleans

Emily D. Langhorne

Like other Rough South writers, Barb Johnson is "not concerned with . . . faded and fallen aristocrats" but instead focuses her writing on the working-class people who make up the world in which she has lived (Johnson, "An Interview with Barb Johnson"). In *More of This World or Maybe Another* (2009), a collection of linked short stories, she offers glimpses into the lives of characters "who are living their lives well beyond the view of the tourist" in the "sweet dark heart" of a working-class New Orleans neighborhood (Johnson, "An Interview"). The collection centers on the life of Delia Delahoussaye, beginning at a high school dance in rural Louisiana and ending over two decades later in New Orleans. While many characters reappear frequently throughout the stories, Delia is the epicenter of the collection, and her presence ties the stories together.

Because of Johnson's focus on working-class southerners, she has found a place in the Rough South canon; however, Louisiana bears little cultural resemblance to the rest of the American South. "The vibe in New Orleans is much more European and African than Southern," Johnson explains ("An Interview"). In the same interview, Johnson calls New Orleans a place of "utter separateness from the work-hard-and-get-ahead culture of the rest of the United States. Which is not to say that we don't work hard. We do. Harder than most, frankly, because all our economic eggs are in the tourism basket, and that setup requires a permanent underclass to make it work. And that permanent underclass is well acquainted with the lack of connection between working hard and getting ahead." As members of this permanent underclass and products of this mixed ancestry, Johnson's characters—with their "kinky blonde hair" and "dark skin and light eyes"—are well aware that the work-hard-get-ahead rules of the American dream don't apply to their world (*More of This World*, 141). This knowledge imbues her characters with the laissez-faire attitude that permeates New Orleans, in Johnson's view. They have a deep-seated belief that nothing will ever really change, but they don't view their situation as hopeless; after all, there's beer in the fridge, football on TV, and a crawfish boil later ("An Interview"). Because of this attitude, Johnson's characters aren't filled with rage over class bias. They might make fun of the students at "rich kids' college Uptown," but they aren't overly concerned with the prejudices against the working class (*More of This World*, 65). For the most part, they don't attempt to escape their working-class community; instead, they seek to find belonging within it.

In this respect, Johnson's work is deeply concerned with a fundamental aspect of the American dream: American individualism. Johnson's characters search for their individual authenticity—"the moral guideline of being true to one's own, unique self; of realizing a core self unhindered by societal forces"—that is unmistakably American in its nature (Kis, "American Dream").

As Truslow Adams explains, the American dream is "not a dream of motor cars and high wages merely" but also a dream of people being "recognized by others for what they are" (quoted in Kis, "American Dream"). At its center, the American dream stresses individualism over conventionalism. Katalin Kis explains: "The American Dream unmistakably embraces the ideal of individual authenticity. . . . [It] valorizes authentic personhood, the unique individual who shall be able to thrive in their very own way."

Johnson's characters undergo psychological stress as they battle between possessing individual authenticity and navigating working-class expectations about sexuality, gender roles, and religion. In many of her stories, the conflict centers on characters' internal struggle to accept their true selves in the face of these expectations. Theirs is not a struggle against class bias but rather a struggle to carve out space for their individual authenticity within their working-class environment.

The opening scene of *More of This World or Maybe Another* is distinctly American in its setting: a Sadie Hawkins dance in a high school gym in rural Louisiana. It's a place of clearly defined gender roles—"Boys in one group. Girls in another" (9)—and class structure: "Everyone knew everyone, and it had already been decided three generations ago which people you'd invite to your house and which people you'd never get to know" (31).

The gym resembles a barnyard of creatures that lack agency over their lives. Delia's classmates maintain a pack mentality. The boys bark at girls and puff their chests out at each other, signifying their desires for sex and violence. When it's time for a dance, the "hoop-earring-and-eyeliner catpack" (7) of girls "scatter like buckshot, snagging boys to dance with" (3). While Delia feels disgusted that her "whole class has turned into a bunch of cattle for how they only do what everyone else is doing" (7), she, too, has resigned herself to a life predetermined by her environment, knowing that she will "likely have to marry one of the idiots" in the gym, even though she will hate her life after she does it (5).

Internally, however, Delia struggles between this resignation and embracing her authentic individuality. She dreams of places with stoplights "where the night doesn't press down on you the way it's pressing down on her now, like it's water she might drown in if she doesn't pay attention" (13). She conflates her sexual yearnings with her desperation to escape rural Louisiana when, in fact, Delia's claustrophobia has less to do with her physical surroundings than with her internal struggle over her sexual identity. Delia knows she wants other things but can't name them. She is worried she won't recognize them if she sees them (2). Accepting her homosexuality is the only means through which Delia can find her authentic personhood and learn to name these things.

On the night of the dance, Delia and Charlene, who goes by Chuck, flee the gym and drive to "Emerald City," an old oil refinery. There Delia has the opportunity to accept her true self. While she internally acknowledges both the sexual tension and her longing for Chuck, readers can assume she misses the chance to unlock her authentic personhood by failing to act on these desires. Although the story's ending is ambiguous ("Delia will lean in for a kiss or turn away" [18]), readers feel her hesitation ("Now. Or Now") and next encounter her three years later, living in New Orleans with her fiancé, Calvin, Chuck's twin brother, the boy she never wanted to date.

Chuck, on the other hand, accepts who she is. In two uncollected stories, "Beggars and Choosers" and "Rider," Johnson reveals that, during high school, Chuck too struggled with her identity. She pretended to be like the other girls who "like what they're supposed to like," while secretly believing that the "wrong song" played inside her because she was in love with her classmate Janie Lowell ("Rider"). Exhausted from denying her sexuality—and by extension her authentic individuality—Chuck sets out for San Francisco immediately after graduation. There Chuck begins a relationship with a woman named Jin. When Chuck sends photos home, Delia notices that "Chuck looks different than [she] remembers. Happier, she guesses." Understanding and accepting herself, Chuck has embraced her authentic personhood and becomes capable of pursuing her individual happiness, another fundamental aspect of the American dream.

Conversely, after high school, Delia is still trapped in a heterosexual relationship that is heading toward marriage, and she continues to experience unrest and unhappiness. While the environment of rural Louisiana may have been confining, Delia's inability to acknowledge her true self has kept her trapped long after she has "escaped" to New Orleans. Relocating did not cure her anxieties, because they stem from her inner turmoil over whether to resign herself to, or reject, a life in which she will forever deny both her sexuality and her true self. Her thoughts about the catfish Calvin has caught underscore her thoughts about life with Calvin: "There's a frantic splashing in the bucket next to Delia, and she's sure one of the fish is about to jump out and swim away. The struggle doesn't last, though. The catfish go quiet in their murky prison. They've accepted their fate, Delia imagines. *Que sera, sera*" (*More of This World*, 24).

However, after Delia meets Maggie, she is capable of feeling connected and happy. She stops "shaving away pieces of herself," which she claims to have been doing "to make Calvin fit into the picture" (35). However, Calvin is not to blame for this shaving away; it comes from Delia's contorting herself into a heteronormative role, which forces her to suppress her individual authenticity—beginning with her sexuality and extending into other areas of her life, like her love of reading. She begins to understand this denial of self as the true source of her unhappiness: "She wonders if her crankiness . . . might be from having to listen to the shaved pieces of herself shouting at her *WakeUpWakeUpWakeUp*" (35). As she develops an intimate relationship with Maggie, Delia begins to "wake up." Finding her authentic personhood, she happily spends the next twenty years running the laundromat, providing a community hub and place of belonging for the misfits of her working-class New Orleans neighborhood (160).

Delia's two romantic interests act as her foils. Because of their backgrounds, neither Calvin nor Maggie struggles with a sense of self. As a heterosexual male and the epitome of masculinity in working-class society, Calvin "isn't much bothered by other people's assumptions. Calvin's okay with Calvin, so Calvin's okay with the world. He fits in everywhere" (32). He remains at ease even among the college-educated city kids. Likewise, because of her privileged upbringing, Maggie assumes acceptance in any social circle she enters. Even when she first meets Delia and behaves rudely, Maggie knows no embarrassment; instead she acts "like suddenly she's a part of things" (27).

Like Delia, two of the collection's other protagonists, Dooley and Pudge, also struggle to realize their individual authenticities. In both rural Louisiana and working-class New Orleans, traditional notions about masculinity prevail, creating difficulties for these sensitive, young male protagonists. They "grapple as little boys with the links between manhood and violence," and their sensibilities isolate them from others in their environment (Stinson). Dooley and Pudge experience emotional confusion as they attempt to reconcile who they truly are—sensitive and thoughtful young men—and the societal expectations of what a man should be: tough, protective, stoic. They cannot act on their individual authenticity while simultaneously conforming to the expectations of their environment. Stifling their authentic personhoods damages their ability to become fully actualized people and ultimately hinders their ability to pursue individual happiness.

Even as a young boy, Dooley, Delia's younger brother, emanates a gentle disposition. In "If the Holy Spirit Comes for You," he is developing a private morality that conflicts with the expectations of his society as well as his Catholic upbringing: he has "learned that the Holy Spirit will give you the courage to do what you need to do in life. . . . Recently, though, he's been wondering if maybe killing is wrong" *(More of This World,* 42). His moral dilemma arises because he lacks the courage or desire to go hunting with his uncles. His uncles try to force him to participate in this male rite of passage on his thirteenth birthday, but after talking with his older brother, "who went off to war to shoot at strangers, [and] now lives downriver on a houseboat that he never leaves" (42), Dooley decides he is "not going to shoot anything, next week or ever" (45).

Dooley's interests lie in less "masculine" pursuits. He loves music, which pulls "at the soft parts in [his] chest, a vibrating good feeling" (47), and he once took apart a clock on the mantel "just to see what made it go" (48); however,

Dooley cannot embrace his authentic personhood because the gender roles of rural Louisiana confine him to traditional notions of manhood, which his uncles embody. He longs for their acceptance, as demonstrated by his joy over being included in the roughhousing of the football game, but he is too afraid of rejection to reveal his true self and to seek an acceptance based on his individualism.

While Dooley's sensitivity isolates him from his uncles, it also gives him the ability to understand them. He does not resent their actions, because he values their intentions. He understands that they want to do something to make his birthday special, "and hunting is special to them" (42). He recognizes that they are trying to help him become a man, according to rural Louisiana's definition of masculinity, and he knows it is "hard for them to see how other people are. . . . People who aren't like them" (46).

Although Dooley escapes the hunting trip, his uncles test his manhood by forcing him to slaughter a piglet, the runt of the litter, which Dooley has been trying to save and for which he has felt great affection. Ultimately, Dooley's "hand does what the Holy Spirit requires, but Dooley doesn't watch. . . . It's some other boy and some other hand pushing the point of the knife in" (58). His uncles "slap the other boy's back and say excited things" while "the real Dooley opens and closes his bloody hands, concentrates entirely on the sticky sound" (58). Dooley has betrayed his individual authenticity; he has allowed the values of others, rather than his own values, to dictate his actions. He has shifted his morality to comply with an image constructed by others rather than reveal his true self.

Nine years later, Dooley is living in New Orleans with his wife, Tina, and their three-year-old daughter, Gracie, when his manhood, from a traditional standpoint, comes under attack: Tina informs him that their daughter is not his biological child. Dooley, however, reacts to the news with introspection rather than anger. Regardless of who her biological father is, Dooley believes Gracie is his daughter, and he will not abandon her. Ironically, his efforts to protect Gracie result in her death. Although he takes several protective measures—he "tugs the metal slide out of her fist so she won't hurt herself. He rolls the windows up, leaving a couple of inches for air, then locks the doors"—Gracie dies of heatstroke while napping in his truck while he is in a store, buying her a safer car seat (105).

Dooley's internal monologue reveals his need to discuss Gracie's death and seek atonement, but he fails to do so. Instead his internalized grief leads to erratic behavior, including sneaking into the house of his affluent neighbor, a man whose grand house symbolizes the wealth and power traditionally associated with manhood and contrasts Dooley's state as a broken man.

Eleven years later, when readers next encounter him, Dooley seems carefree, but Delia reveals that the previous year, on the tenth anniversary of Gracie's death, "Dooley went into a tailspin and ended up on the psych ward at Charity" (152). Despite outward appearances, Dooley's inability to work through his tragedy has halted his personal development. At the age of thirty-three, he spends all night at the bar, and the next morning he is "still crackling with energy from his gig last night, maybe from other things, too" (140). Dooley's story is a tragic one, not only because of his daughter's death, but also because, from an early age, he repressed his true self, fearing the judgment of others. As an adult, he has failed in his search for authenticity, for he cannot progress after his tragedy, instead regressing, behaving like an adolescent.

Like Dooley, Pudge too has a sensitive disposition as a youth: "Nice things make him cry" (77). His violent father and others in his working-class New Orleans community equate this sensitivity with weakness. Pudge's peers tease him, calling him a "titty baby" when he cries. As an adult, Pudge dismisses his sister's suggestion that "his nickname, Pudge, has shaped him, tied him irrevocably to the pain of his childhood" (125). In truth, he has internalized others' assumptions about who he is; for instance, Delia reveals that at parties, Pudge always sings "Danny Boy": "He's actually developed a nice arrangement for it, but he always cries halfway through the old-fashioned song. Someone always brings him a beer then. And everyone calls his name, *Pudge! Pudge!* Every time, he laughs, makes fun of himself. *Crying like a goddamn titty baby*" (161).

The childhood insult has become the way he views himself. Lacking in confidence, Pudge has fulfilled others' prophecies about him; for instance, his parents had no faith in his ability, and now, fifteen years later, he is an unemployed alcoholic.

Pudge has an adolescent son, Luis, but Luis's mother, Deysi, has told him that his father died in a war. Deysi's lie wounds Pudge so deeply that he adopts her opinion of his unworthiness to be a father: "Luis is twelve, nearly grown. Why blow it for the kid is what Pudge figures" (121). Although Pudge lacks the full picture of Luis's home life, he knows that Deysi is living with her drug-dealing boyfriend, Junior, and Luis often sleeps in an abandoned BMW in a dangerous part of the neighborhood. Pudge searches for get-rich-quick schemes and makes excuses for his behavior, but he never really attempts to make a change, overcome his addiction, and provide stability for Luis. Lacking individual authenticity, Pudge remains incapable of taking control of his life. He longs to tell Luis the truth, but he lacks the self-confidence to do anything more than secretly leave Luis his dog tags. As a result, Pudge perpetuates a cycle of "fatherless boys trapped in a maze" ("Meet Barb Johnson," 4). Delia and Maggie look after Luis as best they can, just as Pudge's Aunt Alma and her partner Big Luce did for him. Pudge's weaknesses come not from his sensitive nature but from his inability to feel confident about his identity in the face of external judgment. Having abandoned his search for authentic personhood, he is a stagnant human, lost in a maze of addiction, indecision, and inaction.

The end of Johnson's collection showcases darker elements of the working-class neighborhood. Although poverty and violence have been the backdrop against which these stories are set, graphic sexual and physical abuse are at the forefront of "St. Luis of Palmyra," as Luis attempts to navigate and escape his circumstances. While Luis has already developed a cynical view of the world—"The same losers win everything because the good stuff gets jacked before you can get to it"—he also believes that he can improve life for him and his mother if he becomes a man (170). For him, Catholic confirmation becomes a symbol of that possibility. Luis attempts to understand how Christian morality applies to his life and resorts to rationalization when thinking about his behavior, as in his stealing from Junior: "If Junior's gonna hit him whether he's done anything or not . . . he might as well take a little payment for it" (172). Luis steals a catechism book from a girl in his class after he loses his, believing she will get confirmed automatically because girls are good. At lunch, he steals a sandwich for his mama because grilled cheese is her favorite. As Scott Doyle asserts in his review of Johnson's collection, Luis is struggling to "shape a private morality under challenging circumstances."

Because of the ease with which he commits such petty crimes, Luis appears to be following the same life trajectory as Junior, but Luis actually expresses authentic individuality because he is holding on to his core self in the face of extreme circumstances. Luis's core self is defined by his love for those who treat him with love: his mother, Abuelita, Maggie, and Delia. Luis yields to Junior's sexual demands out of fear for his mother's safety. He helps Delia and Maggie decorate for their anniversary party. He offers to miss his catechism class, and thereby forgo his chance at the confirmation he desperately desires, so that he can stay with his mother after Junior breaks her arm.

In the final assignment for catechism class, Luis makes up a "new kind of saint": Saint Luis of Palmyra (179). Saint Luis will help "himself and his family and not wait around and see if the bad people are stop being bad" (173). Luis, concerned above all else with protecting his mother, explains to Father Ben, "'Saints can't be so lazy anymore. . . . They gotta deal'" (179). Unlike Pudge, Luis possesses a strong sense of self. Embracing this core self sometimes results in extreme and morally questionable actions, like drugging Junior to ensure that Abuelita can throw a confirmation party. Nevertheless, it gives Luis agency and provides him with the confidence necessary to break out of the cycle of hopelessness that permeates his world—not necessarily to find a life beyond the neighborhood surrounding Palmyra Street, but a more fulfilling life within it, as Delia, Maggie, and others have done.

Luis's story, and with it Johnson's collection, ends with Luis watching a television show about building bridges. Luis "can't imagine how anyone could make a way to get over all that mess," but by the end of the show, a bridge has been built across the river and rocks (185). In Johnson's working-class New Orleans community, the acceptance of one's individual authenticity and the relationships that become possible after that acceptance are a lot like the bridge Luis so admires: a way of getting over all the mess and building a road to a meaningful life.

Works Cited

Doyle, Scott. "*More of This World or Maybe Another.*" *Short Review*. https://www.theshortreview.com/reviews/BarbJohnsonMoreofThisWorldorMaybeAnother.htm. Accessed September 25, 2018.

Johnson, Barb. "Beggars and Choosers." *Baltimore Review*, Summer 2017. https://baltimore review.org/index.php/summer_2017/contributor/barb-johnson. Accessed September 25, 2018.

Johnson, Barb. "For the Good Lies." In *Don't Quit Your Day Job*, edited by Sonny Brewer. Kindle ed. MP Publishing, 2010.

Johnson, Barb. "An Interview with Barb Johnson." Interview with Andrew Scott. *Hobart*, March 27, 2013. https://www.hobartpulp.com/web_features/an-interview-with-barb-johnson. Accessed September 15, 2018.

Johnson, Barb. "Meet Barb Johnson." In *More of This World or Maybe Another*, 2–4. Harper Perennial, 2009.

Johnson, Barb. *More of This World or Maybe Another*. Harper Perennial, 2009.

Johnson, Barb. "Rider." *Yemassee* 20, no.1 (2013): 35–39.

Kiernan, Jacob. "Little Punch Somewhere Soft: An Interview with Barb Johnson." *New Orleans Review*, n.d. https://www.neworleansreview.org/little-punch-somewhere-soft-an-interview-with-barb-johnson. Accessed September 25, 2018.

Kis, Kaitlin. "The American Dream of Authentic Personhood: Homosexuality, Class, and the Normative Individual in the U.S. Queer Male Impostor Films (1970–2009)." *European Journal of American Studies* 11, no. 3 (2017). https://journals.openedition.org/ejas/11740. Accessed October 7, 2018.

Stinson, Susan. "*More of This World or Maybe Another* by Barb Johnson." *Lambda Literary*, March 9, 2010. https://www.lambdaliterary.org/reviews/fiction/03/09/more-of-this-world -or-maybe-another-by-barb-johnson. Accessed September 25, 2018.

Born in 1965, the novelist **Inman Majors** was raised in suburban Knoxville, Tennessee. Son of a longtime political lobbyist and
nephew to Johnny Majors, head football coach of first the University
of Pittsburgh and then the University of Tennessee, Majors gained
insights to the inner workings of politics as well as upper-division
college football. Majors earned a BA from Vanderbilt and an MFA
from the University of Alabama and lives in Charlottesville, Virginia,
with his wife and son. For many years he was a professor of English
at James Madison University.

"I Ought to Have Worn Overalls"

The Novels of Inman Majors in the Millennial South

Scott D. Yarbrough

Inman Majors's South is not the history-chained South of Faulkner or the Christ-haunted South of O'Connor; it is instead a South that in a fifty-year period had transformed from a largely rural agricultural culture to a suburban industrial culture. Nor is his South the Rough South of meth dealers and trailer park domestic disputes as displayed in the works of Wiley Cash or William Gay. Majors's milieu is the South of the cultural crossroads, and his characters are often people stricken by the choices afforded them in millennial America, men and women who are unsure where to turn.

In mainstream American literature, writers growing up a generation after World War II found themselves living in a different kind of nation from the one their parents and grandparents had known. With the expansion of the highway system, the installation of interstates, and the proliferation of the automobile, the cities and towns of the United States began growing outward in familiar patterns: a ring of suburbs, followed by a ring of industry, followed by further rings of suburbs. Terms like "suitcase city" and "bedroom community" entered the lexicon. Middle-class Americans began living not in a city known for certain characteristics but near that city in a suburb largely devoid of identity and character. As Gertrude Stein famously said of Oakland, California, as it went through an early iteration of this process, "There is no there there."

And so a generation of American writers who came of age in the late 1950s through the 1960s tried to confront the growing rootlessness and lack of place in American culture as exemplified by urban expansion and suburban development. Writers who are identified with what is sometimes called "suburban realism" include John Updike, John Cheever, and Richard Yates. Tellingly, all these writers hailed from the Northeast: Pennsylvania, Massachusetts, and New York, respectively. Although Majors's books do not particularly echo the works of these *New Yorker* writers, they deal with similar issues, a generation or two later, from a pronounced southern perspective. Southern literature has always been about place, first and foremost, and so the loss of a sense of home, of place, is all the more pronounced in works about the South.

Other prevalent motifs that appear throughout his novels seem drawn from Majors's background and experience. His characters sometimes have family connections that do not help to establish the protagonists in society so much as set unrealistic expectations before them. Politics and political machinations frame and inform his second and third novels, *Wonderdog* and *The Millionaires*. Similarly, his fourth book, *Love's Winning Plays*, sheds light on the inner workings, traditions, and foibles of a nameless SEC football team.

Significantly, an important component of Majors's work is humor. The arc of at least three of his five novels is comedic, and both his portrayal of Jason Sayer's dark night of the soul in *Swimming in Sky* and his presentation of the complex political machinations and intensive character studies in *The Millionaires* are leavened by a wry sense of humor. As a southern writer, Majors is influenced not so much by southern progenitors like Faulkner and O'Connor as he is by the lyrical works of F. Scott Fitzgerald and the dry hilarity of the British novelist P. G. Wodehouse (Reddick, "Inman Majors's Novel"). Indisputably, Robert Penn Warren's *All the King's Men* (1946) stands as an antecedent to *The Millionaires*, but Majors's style owes very little to Warren's. Hasty reviewers have occasionally likened Majors's writing to Cormac McCarthy's, but with the possible exception of McCarthy's comic Knoxville novel *Suttree* (1979), these comparisons seem largely rooted in Majors's similar eschewing of quotation marks and the fact that both men hail from Knoxville.

Majors's first novel, *Swimming in Sky* (2000), tells the story of a season of melancholy in the life of Jason Sayer, a twenty-five-year-old man from Knoxville. Just as Majors's uncle is a famous football coach, Sayer's uncle

was a famous player at the University of Tennessee with a statue dedicated
to him. The narrator, Sayer, is in both emotional and spiritual retreat. He
is unemployed and living with his mother and her equally unemployed if
affable boyfriend. He is somewhat unhinged from a bad experience with
hallucinogenic drugs, and he has visions of "shadows" that seem to haunt him
and stalk him and bring on panic attacks. Witty and sensitive, but with some
particularly rough edges, he is trying to discern some direction for his life.
Sayer will establish a pattern for most of Majors's subsequent protagonists:
Dev Degraw of *Wonderdog*, Raymond Love of *Love's Winning Plays*, and
Penelope Lemon of the eponymous *Penelope Lemon: Game On!*

Sayer's paranoid and traumatized thoughts in the wake of his drug
experience seem to have taken on spiritual dimensions, perhaps because
the experience happened on Good Friday, but more likely because his friends
prod him with strange comments of a religious nature. For example, his
friend Bobsmith (an elided nickname) keeps asking Jason in the midst of his
"bad trip" about Christ and the betrayal of Judas. The narrator's experience
serves as a clear metaphor for a spiritual crisis of faith he is undergoing, a
crisis not necessarily born of religious faith, although the crisis is signified as
such in the narrative. For example, he turns to the Bible to calm himself down
at times, and it becomes clear that Beth, who has interested him, is serious
about her faith. In Sayer's case, religious faith seems to act as synecdoche,
indicating a broader lack of faith in himself and the world around him. His
malaise is matched by other physical afflictions; he needs a knee operation
that he can't afford. Jason's life is mirrored by that of his mother's boyfriend
Tom, who is himself in the middle of an emotional crisis that proves to be
connected to a serious health problem. Jason will eventually realize that
perhaps his friends are not trustworthy and are manipulating him for their
own entertainment as well.

Jason Sayer's grandfather Ray is a minor character in the novel, but he
embodies one of Majors's greater themes. They have a fragile relationship,
since the grandfather requires Jason to show a certain level of submissiveness,
and Jason is largely unable to provide it. Raised on a farm, Ray now sells real
estate; he accompanies Jason in meeting the orthopedist who will operate
on Jason's knee, and dickers over the price of the surgery. Playing the part of
the dignified country naïf, Ray convinces the doctor to come down on the
rates, saying to Jason, "By god, I ought to have worn overalls" (83). In that one
sentence—a knowledge of his roots, a knowledge of the world before him,

and a resentment of people from other places or different classes who would presume to judge and underestimate those born in the rural South—we see Majors's most significant themes at work.

Majors's first foray into political fiction occurs in his second novel, *Wonderdog* (2004). The novel is more comedic than *Swimming in Sky* in both tone and structure; its protagonist, Dev Degraw, is, like Jason Sayer, a bit aimless and unsure what to do with himself. He similarly comes from a divorced family and similarly has connections to celebrity: his father is a multiterm Democratic governor of Alabama. Dev himself had a brief taste of celebrity as a child actor in *Bayou Dog*, a television show that positioned itself as a cross between animal-based family dramas such as *Lassie*, *Gentle Ben*, and *Flipper*; the show only lasted one year. The show's short run does not stop the man who played Degraw's rough-and-tumble sheriff-father, Clay Kingston, from trying to stage a reunion and perhaps make a comeback, despite Dev's great reluctance.

Dev Degraw tells the reader in the opening line of *Wonderdog*, "Like everyone else in the world I am a lawyer" (3). The reader perhaps makes immediate associations: privilege, connections, and a hefty bank balance. However, like Jason Sayer, Degraw is in existential crisis, poised at a point of emotional transition. He has largely failed one of his last clients, he is looking for comfort in meaningless sexual trysts, and he shirks responsibility wherever he can. Recently divorced, he shares custody of his small daughter but has difficulty keeping up his child support. He tries to avoid being made into a political operative for his father and spends as much time as he can haunting the bars of Tuscaloosa, trying to recoup gambling losses, and flirting with his daughter's teacher. He is pushed throughout the novel by the people in his life; these attempts at motivation occur subtly at times and not so subtly when it comes to his father's longtime African American friend and political fixer, Sam Shade. Like the others, Shade wants Dev to reengage with his life; more than the rest, Shade wants him to use his native abilities and take up a career in politics like his father. *Wonderdog*'s mode is primarily satirical, and as he does in many of his works, Majors pokes fun at many of the South's sacred cows.

Majors's third novel, *The Millionaires* (2009), is his most significant work, and it is not an exaggeration to say it is one of the most ambitious and accomplished American novels written in the last quarter century. Set initially in the late 1970s, the lengthy novel tells the story of the Cole brothers, two bankers from Glennville, Tennessee (a fictional approximation of Knoxville), who have big plans: the younger, Roland, intends to run for governor with the help of his irascible older brother J. T., and the two of them together plan to bring the 1983 World's Fair to Glennville. The Cole brothers are based on Jake Butcher and C. H. Butcher Jr., Knoxville bankers who succeeded in bringing the World's Fair to Knoxville in 1982 before running into trouble for bank fraud (Hoffman, "Southern Comfort"). Roland and J. T. are prefigured in fiction by earlier searchers for an elusive and illusory American dream, such as Jay Gatsby and Willie Stark. Like these characters, the brothers Cole come from blue-collar roots and are willing to use less-than-legal means to achieve their goals. Discussing the novel's genesis in an interview, Majors stated, "One of the primary themes is that the South in the late seventies and early eighties was a region in transition, moving as it was from an area dominated by farms and small towns to one where the city and suburb reign supreme." He goes on to explain:

> For a long time I've wanted to write a book about my parents' generation, those people who just preceded the baby boomers. Three of my four grandparents were raised on farms in Tennessee. . . . My parents, however, were raised in small Tennessee towns like Huntland and Winchester. And I was raised in the city of Knoxville. I grew up skateboarding in the suburbs and going to malls and things like that but I also spent a lot of time in small Tennessee towns when I'd go to visit my grandparents. ("Interview with Lacey Galbraith")

Both *The Great Gatsby* and *All the King's Men* are constructed on similar narrative models: a first-person narrator tells the tale of a more heroically figured protagonist whose rise and fall follows the arc of Aristotelian tragedy. *The Millionaires* is more complex, however. It is told largely in the third person, although certain chapters (echoing Joyce's *Ulysses*) are related in dramatic form rather than through narrative, and other chapters take the form of lists or a collection of vignettes. *The Millionaires* has four protagonists: Roland and J. T. Cole, lobbyist and fixer Mike Teague, and, most significantly, J. T.'s wife, Corrine. The younger Cole is more evolved, perhaps, although there are depths to J. T. hidden by a charming good-ole-boy mask. Their father was a small-town store owner turned banker, and the two have become bankers on a large scale, with many branches in many cities. Mike Teague is perhaps the moral center of the book. While his cynical wiliness may remind readers of Warren's Jack Burden, Teague's innate integrity and decency recall Fitzgerald's Nick Carraway. Teague's story is more central to the novel than Carraway's is in *The Great Gatsby*. Teague's quiet reasonableness provides insights into the Coles' actions.

When Roland discusses with Teague his need to bring the World's Fair to Knoxville after he has failed in his bid for governor, he explains that he is not interested in the money for money's sake; instead, he says, "I'm talking about being in the game. Beating *them at their game*. A game they don't think you've even got a right to play. I didn't like getting the high hat when I used to come up here with Daddy to the bank conventions. It stuck in my craw a bit" (331).

Although portrayed in living and breathing detail, the Cole brothers are familiar figures in American literature, harkening back as they do to Willie Stark and Jay Gatsby. And Teague, as mentioned earlier, recalls Nick Carraway and Jack Burden. But Corrine Cole is rendered in exquisite detail, a thoroughly three-dimensional character beside whom Daisy Buchanan and Anne Stanton seem pale objects in comparison. Along with Teague, Corrine Cole is in many ways the beating heart of the novel. Just as hungry as J. T. and Roland, and from just as humble origins, in important ways she has remembered the old southern adage: don't forget where you come from. She recognizes when J. T. is cheating on her and stands up to him, once drunkenly crashing a car into the bungalow where he is enjoying a tryst with a lover. The Coles are eventually brought low when they are caught engaging in bank fraud, and eventually their fall also takes on a more tragic aspect. Nevertheless, one of the novel's closing scenes shows Corrine working for a living again behind a jewelry counter at a department store, and it is an important note for the narrative to strike: Corrine is a survivor who will make it through.

As stated earlier, despite the great ambitiousness of *The Millionaires* and its essentially tragic arc, it is still a funny novel, with many dry asides and observations showing again Majors's keen, satirically minded insights. His next two novels are set thoroughly in the comedic realm. Just as Majors's knowledge of his hometown's history and his father's political insights informed *The Millionaires*, so his thorough understanding of the inner workings of big-time SEC college football benefits *Love's Winning Plays*, published in 2012. Raymond Love is a graduate assistant trying to be promoted to a graduate assistant coach. A former quarterback star for a small Division III team, he is scrabbling for purchase in a Division I SEC team with all its attendant politics and complications. He has been dating Brooke (whom he realizes rather after the fact is the athletic director's daughter), and it seems the only way into her life is through a book club where the members read and discuss books like *Feast, Travel, Meditate*, which describes a woman who traveled about Europe by rail and was tutored by a "Belgian yoga teacher named Henri" to "eat what was in season," because the "idea was to live in the moment and to use what was at hand," because "if you meditated, and shopped locally grown, that seemed to take care of a lot of problems" (151–52).

Love is tasked with accompanying a beloved, legendary, but utterly incorrigible defensive line coach known to one and all as Coach Woody on a series of booster outings called the Pigskin Cavalcade. Love is supposed to keep Coach Woody from behaving badly, which is no easy task. Majors seems to be one of the few southern men who can enjoy college football thoroughly and yet not turn it into his primary household religion. Internet gurus obsessed with insider knowledge come under his microscope, as does the ubiquitous high five and the fist bump. At the same time, men who seek to portray themselves as sensitive and in touch with their feminine side (such as Joel, a member of the book club who bakes bread for the meetings) are equally skewered. Unlike Dev Degraw or Jason Sayer, Raymond Love is a centered and balanced individual the reader can root for throughout the novel.

Majors's 2018 novel, *Penelope Lemon: Game On!*, is, like *Love's Winning Play*, a decidedly comedic novel. The novel is the first of a projected series about the titular character; Majors has already published a sequel. Penelope Lemon is in some ways cast in the same mold as Majors's earlier characters Sayer and Degraw. Like them, she is poised at an existential intersection and is not sure which way to turn. She is recently divorced, caring for her nine-year-old son Theo, and she has moved in with her mother and stepfather. Adding insult to injury, she is underemployed at a country-themed restaurant named Coonskins. She is, in other ways, a kind of photo-negative antithesis of Dev Degraw. She does not have a college degree; her divorced husband provided most of the family income; she has no important family connections; and for the most part, Penelope has been led to this place in her life not by bad decisions (with one exception that fuels a subtheme in the plot) but simply by her divorce. Less complex thematically than *Wonderdog*, *Penelope Lemon: Game On!* is nevertheless filled with sardonic observations and barbs about the postmillennial suburban South. There are no farms, no big plantation houses, and little discussion about race, but there are Little

League games, problems with photos taken years earlier in an indiscreet moment appearing on a pornographic website, and the need to protect her son Theo from bullying. Penelope's tactic in the last circumstance is to teach Theo wrestling moves gleaned from watching pro wrestling on television, and her use of this tactic tells the reader much about Penelope's character. Majors continued Penelope's story with a second installment in 2020, *Operation Dimwit: A Penelope Lemon Novel*.

Humor has always played a part in southern literature. It is woven throughout Faulkner's fiction and permeates the best of Welty's stories. One cannot imagine O'Connor's stories without their dark gallows humor, and it is the humor in Walker Percy's fiction that elevates it from mere philosophizing to art. But satire always has a mailed fist inside its velvet glove of wit and whimsy, and in Majors's fiction, the humor strikes home again and again and again. Readers wander into his novels to be entertained by his humor, but they find themselves caught up in the small and significant stories of real people in the real millennial South.

Works Cited

Hoffman, Roy. "Southern Comfort." *New York Times Sunday Book Review*, January 23, 2009, 19.

Majors, Inman. "Airing It Out." Interview with Lacey Galbraith. *Chapter 16*, January 13, 2010. https://chapter16.org/airing-it-out. Accessed August 20, 2018.

Majors, Inman. *Love's Winning Plays*. Norton, 2012.

Majors, Inman. *The Millionaires*. Norton, 2009.

Majors, Inman. *Penelope Lemon: Game On!* Yellow Shoe Fiction. Louisiana State University Press, 2018.

Majors, Inman. *Swimming in Sky*. Southern Methodist University Press, 2000.

Majors, Inman. *Wonderdog*. St. Martin's, 2004.

Reddick, Niles. "Inman Majors's Novel *Penelope Lemon: Game On!*: A Review and Interview." *Tuck Magazine*, August 7, 2018. http://www.tuckmagazine.com. Accessed August 20, 2018.

Joe Samuel "Sam" Starnes was born in Alabama but grew up in Cedartown, Georgia. He has a bachelor's degree from the University of Georgia, an MA from Rutgers University in Newark, New Jersey, and an MFA in Creative Nonfiction from Goucher College. He was awarded a fellowship to the 2006 Sewanee Writers' Conference. His first novel, *Calling*, was published in 2005 and reissued in 2014 as an e-book. The novel *Fall Line*, added to the *Atlanta Journal-Constitution*'s "Best of the South" list, was published by NewSouth Books in 2011. *Red Dirt: A Tennis Novel* was released in 2015 to favorable reviews. His journalistic pieces have appeared in the *New York Times, Washington Post, Philadelphia Inquirer*, and various magazines. His short stories and poems have appeared in several literary journals. Since 2000 he has lived in either New Jersey or Philadelphia.

Joe Samuel Starnes
A Devoted Disciple of the Rough South Gospel

Kevin Catalano

In "Larry Brown: Mentor from Afar," Joe Samuel Starnes recounts the moment his writing soul was "saved" by the teachings of the prophets of Rough South literature:

> I learned a lot from [Larry Brown], and one of the most important things is that to be a writer . . . [all] you have to have is the desire to live in the real world, to read everything you can get your hands on, learn from it, and when it comes to writing, the desire to do it, and the determination—as Harry Crews said and Brown took heed—"to keep your ass in the chair." (16)

Nearly every writer has an author he or she emulates and is inspired by, but few keep their asses in the seat of their mentors' church as faithfully as Starnes. Like a devoted disciple abiding by the Word of the Rough South Gospel, Starnes's three novels, *Calling* (2005), *Fall Line* (2011), and *Red Dirt* (2015), adhere to the commandments laid out by Crews and Brown: his writing focuses on working-class characters with strong ties to home and problems with the bottle; in lush and vivid prose, he both sanctifies the rural landscape and reveals its brutality; and collectively, his books and their characters speak to larger American themes by using the South as a kind of antithesis, southerners as underdogs out to achieve their southern American dream.

As if eager to show his teachers what he can do, Starnes blazes onto the Rough South scene with a fierce debut in *Calling*. Here we have two men on a Greyhound bus: Timber Goodman, a radio man from Louisiana, who is returning home after sabotaging a successful career with booze, married women, and gambling; and Ezekiel Blizzard, a fiery reverend from Georgia, who is fleeing the scene of a gruesome murder. Both are bound by their southern heritage, their rural, working-class backgrounds, and their complicated relationships with the Southern Baptist church. Throughout the novel, which gives equal time to the long and corrupted paths that bring these men together on the bus, we see how Timber and Blizzard are constantly tempted, how they almost always give in to their rapacious desires, and how they both fall from great heights. Much of the twisted pleasure the reader gets from following these characters arises from being witness to their failures. In this way, we see Starnes following the Gospel according to Larry Brown, to whom Starnes dedicated *Calling* and about whom he has written two telling essays. In one, "Larry Brown: A Firefighter Finds His Voice," Starnes observes about Brown's writing, "Characters who drink more than is good for them, as Brown often did, populate his work, and beer and liquor frequently fuel characters' bad decisions" (53). The same is true for Timber in *Calling*, who, if not for his insatiable thirst, would have remained the celebrity disc jockey with "a morning drive-time slot in Houston's biggest country station in the oil boom days, a time when people threw $100 bills around Texas like floppy tortillas" (2). However, Timber lost that job when, drunk on the air, he insulted the station's biggest advertiser and made crude on-air advances toward the married morning newswoman. From this point, Timber lands other radio jobs, promises himself that this time he will stay away from the bottle, succeeds for a few months, and then inevitably falls back into "drinking more than is good for him." As Starnes writes, Timber "had been so high up the ladder at one time, only to fall so far and so fast" (171). That is the tragic fate of many characters from the Rough South: if they get to the top, it won't take long for their thirst to knock them down again.

This pattern also plays itself out in Reverend Blizzard, but in a far more dramatic way. For twenty years, he works his way up to become a successful preacher of his own church, filling the pews with fawning practitioners. He is faithful to his wife and three children, and he avoids the temptations of drink and women. But Starnes's characters cannot be so easily contented: Blizzard "should have been perfectly happy with the use of a private fishing pond, the parish house rent-free, a family that loved him, a wife who cooked and cleaned and raised the kids and earned a steady income teaching school" (*Calling*, 89). Starnes is setting up the pins for the colossal crash. First, Blizzard takes to robbing banks, and then he falls for the sheriff's daughter, a young woman seeking the good preacher's guidance after a period of reckless debauchery in Los Angeles. Much like Timber, Blizzard gives in to the temptations of alcohol and a beautiful woman, which has disastrous consequences, stealing away everything Blizzard had spent so long earning: his family, his church, his soul. The preacher stumbles, but he still has much farther to fall. In the novel's gory climax, in the wild throes of an LSD trip, Reverend Blizzard, crazed and deluded and feeling called by the Lord, kidnaps, tortures, sexually assaults, and then crucifies a victim he believes he is saving. The bold nature of this scene, and others like it, calls to mind those graphic southern novels of the seventies like Harry Crews's *A Feast of Snakes* and Cormac McCarthy's *Child of God*. These were, arguably, the roughest of the Rough South novels. Alongside his admiration of Brown, Starnes acknowledges the influence of Crews, saying of *Feast*, "[It's] as raw and brutal and dark and hilarious as fiction can get. It's a book that is a little too rough for some" ("Mentor from Afar," 13). Nevertheless, Starnes, with the release of *Calling*, firmly establishes himself as an authentic voice of twenty-first-century Rough South literature.

Whereas in *Calling*, Starnes takes the reader all over the country, spanning decades, packing in numerous characters and plot points, in his second novel, *Fall Line*, he slows the pace to focus on one small Georgia town for a single twenty-four-hour period in 1955, on the day that the dam will open to create a lake. Selected for the *Atlanta-Constitution*'s Best Books of the South in 2012, *Fall Line* is both a beautiful lament for the old agrarian South and an allegory for its transformation. The kind of South we find in *Fall Line* is gritty, rudderless, and wild, and through the point of view of a dog named Percy, Starnes zooms in on the brutality of the natural landscape. In one vividly telling scene, Percy hunts down and captures a rabbit.

> He bit down into the fur of the fat belly and held the bunny's head with his front paws as his fangs slashed through the cotton lining and into the soft sweet innards. Its insides were warm. A steamy, stinky waft came up as Percy bit off a hunk of guts and fat and meat and ground it in his teeth and swallowed. . . . After the spine he went for the head, crunching the skull and the moist eyeballs popping in his mouth like muscadines, and then after the

skullcap gave way, the sweet taste of the brain that sprayed juice in his mouth
when it cracked open under the force of his molars. (216–17)

The relentlessness of this description is a marvel, an attention to the brutality of
nature that rivals Cormac McCarthy's. It is also noteworthy that Percy's point
of view echoes that of the novel's antihero, Elmer Blizzard, whose view of the
South is one where survival is a fight—where there are no heroes, just survivors.

For Elmer, a character almost as difficult to like as Glen Davis in Brown's
Father and Son, the Old South is akin to the Wild West, where justice is doled
out by people, not the law. After bludgeoning a pulpwooder with a shovel,
Elmer seeks vengeance on state senator Aubrey Terrell, the politician who
spearheaded the plan to flood thousands of acres of land, thus creating Lake
Terrell and modernizing the region with electricity and lucrative lakefront
property. While the locals regard Terrell as a champion of Georgia, in the
background he and his wealthy associates play poker for that property, one
thousand acres a chip. "'You know the rules,' Aubrey said, 'so ante up. One
lake lot to play'" (77). But Elmer, the miserable loner, seems to be the only one
in the novel to despise Terrell, for two reasons: first, when Elmer's parents'
farm was devastated during the Depression, and Elmer's daddy died, Terrell
bought up the family land cheaply; and second, the senator does not respect
the land, or in Elmer's words, he "was a man who did not appreciate what
he had or where he came from" (221). When Elmer tracks down Terrell and
holds him at gunpoint, he makes clear his intentions before killing him: "I'm
upset about my land, my family's land. That's what this is about. It's about the
Finley land that you took. And what you are doing to it" (244).

Starnes echoes this theme of the sanctity of homeland and, correspondingly,
the reluctance for change, through Percy. Ironically, the dog is more articulate
than Elmer in his observations of the changing landscape: "Percy couldn't
get his mind around the way people were acting, the changes in their
routines" (50), and "The land had changed. People had changed. His life had
changed. He couldn't understand it" (103). Similarly, Percy's owner, a widow
who resides in the area soon to be covered by Lake Terrell, tells Elmer, "I
told my daughter up there in Atlanta that it's a bad curse awaits those who
forget where they came from" (208). Through these voices, it is clear that the
novel's position on losing touch with one's homeland is an unwelcome and
grievous change. However, Starnes is a deft, nuanced author, less interested
in allegories and themes than he is in people. Had the novel ended with the

senator's death, *Fall Line* might be considered a bit didactic. In a noir-like twist, just after Elmer kills Terrell, he is shot dead by the sixteen-year-old majorette the senator was screwing. As Elmer dies, Starnes reminds us that the river is flooding the land and there is no stopping it. Lake Terrell will be a reality; the Old South will be underwater, and the Elmers of the region will be washed away, forgotten. The novel ends with the nostalgic, idealized South from Percy's point of view in the afterlife: "Down the hill the river is blue and sparkling and flowing south without impediment beneath the hanging branches of the willow trees" (252). This is the sentimentalized South that Percy and Elmer long for. There is no man-made lake, no human interference, no land grabbing or greed. By offering up these two respective denouements—the Old South that has become an ideal, the New South realized by greedy politicians—Starnes provides a view of the duality of the South, which, in his third book, he extends to the complicated tug-and-pull of these identities reflected in the southerner.

Enter Jaxie Skinner, the working-class hero of *Red Dirt*, a new kind of southerner for the New South. Where Elmer is broken by meanness, fated to self-destruction, and inflexible to change, Jaxie is optimistic and persistent, a southern Odysseus who travels the country, conquering his foes, while learning to appreciate home and family. What is Jaxie's conquest? He plays tennis. *Red Dirt* is a tennis novel; but don't scoff, for not only is it Starnes's most dramatic and mature book, but it fits right into the Rough South tradition and completes the thematic arc through which Starnes gives us his interpretation of the southern version of the American dream. Even the great Barry Hannah, author of his own tennis novel, *The Tennis Handsome* (1983), and Starnes's mentor at the Sewanee Writers' Conference, played a role in *Red Dirt*'s inception, as Starnes explains, "I told him about my idea to write a novel about a tennis player from rural Georgia. . . . He encouraged me, saying that while there was much literary traffic on the South's red dirt roads, there were very few good novels about tennis. . . . Write your tennis novel, he said. So I did" (*Red Dirt*, 349). For readers coming into *Red Dirt* with the assumption that tennis is a rich-person's sport, Starnes quickly corrects that notion:

> Ray and Ricky had told me about a school they competed against up in the mountains of northwest Georgia that had players who wore overalls and camouflage caps, their sole objective to bounce overheads into the gravel parking lot, an act that set off hooting and hollering from the locals, many

who sipped tallboy Budweisers from paper sacks and smoked Marlboros or chewed Red Man, spitting juicy brown streams onto the edge of the court. (47)

The great pleasure and achievement of *Red Dirt* is that it takes a sport that is misperceived as an upper-class country club lobby and situates it in the dirty South, making the protagonist a Georgia boy, an underdog, for whom the reader can't help but root.

In *Red Dirt*, Starnes continues to follow the Gospel of Larry Brown by choosing to glorify rural, working-class characters. Returning to his appreciation of Brown's work, Starnes points out that "depicting blue-collar characters with care and honesty was one of Brown's primary concerns" ("Larry Brown: A Firefighter," 57). In Brown's own words, "I have great sympathy for the good people of the working class. . . . The little man is kept down by the big man, and it's always been that way, and always will probably" (57). From this class injustice, Starnes creates a "little man" character who takes down the metaphorical big man in various ways. For much of the novel, the little man is the rural southerner, the outsider, venturing out into the big cities of America and France. When a teenage Jaxie makes it to his first big tournament near Miami, he, his father, and his coach are big-eyed and out of their element:

Harry was thrilled to be down here at the world's premier junior tournament, strutting around in a new outfit of Fila tennis clothes, cracking jokes, his head sort of bobbing on his shoulders like some sort of Alabama barnyard rooster. This also was a big time for my dad, a man who usually had coffee and sausage-biscuits for breakfast and lunches of bologna sandwiches, all on the side of a half-paved road. (97)

Later in the novel, Jaxie makes it into the French Open. His father comments on the incongruity: "Jaxie and John, two old country boys, walking through Paris" (138). Finally, Jaxie makes it to the US Open in New York City, the pinnacle of Yankeedom in southern literature; he prevails in his impossible run as a late-thirties tennis player making a comeback. In this way, Red Dirt can be read as Starnes's posthumous gift to Brown, for the novel contains so many satisfying moments of the working-class underdog prevailing against the "big man." And yet this is only part of Jaxie's success, for through his father, he learns how to reconnect with his roots.

Jaxie's humble beginnings are established in a beautiful gesture by his bighearted father, who uses a bulldozer to scrape out the family's very own tennis court in their sprawling backyard. Jaxie's father "was not a farmer, but like just about everyone in rural Georgia, an agrarian life was in his blood way on down to the roots of the family tree. His grandparents and great-grandparents had been sharecroppers, before the Depression ushered in the textile mills and ended the era of the dirt farmer. He thought that tennis, like farming, should be done in the dirt" (28). These "roots of the family tree" are the real trophy that Jaxie is vying for, which he comes to appreciate at key moments in his tennis journey. After young Jaxie's loss at the French Open, when he starts drinking, and after the heartbreaking death of his father, Jaxie's estranged mother and sisters want to sell the house and its property. Jaxie takes on an Elmer-like perspective of the land, telling his family, "No, we should keep it. . . . This land has been in Dad's family for generations" (170). Then, at the end of the novel, in the midst of his winning streak at the US Open, Jaxie comes to realize the value of family. In a dream, Jaxie's daddy tells him, "I know, things ended hard . . . I know, but they are family. . . . Y'all are blood. . . . Call your mama, boy" (342). A southerner's roots, according to Starnes, include both family and home, which we know from *Fall Line* to be a value of the Old South. Jaxie's duality, however, which is also Timber's, fulfills a southern, working-class version of the American dream: to make it big outside of the South. The difference between Jaxie and Timber is that Timber's success outside of the South is short-lived, whereas Jaxie excels by playing by his own rules. What Starnes achieves in *Red Dirt*, then, is an optimistic vision of the twenty-first-century southerner, one who "knows what he has, and knows where he's come from."

The undercurrent that runs through Starnes's three novels like the powerful Oogasula River is the motif of southerners leaving or being misplaced, followed by a kind of homecoming. After Timber's repeated failures to regain his radio career, he returns home to Louisiana, meets a local woman, and reopens his daddy's radio station. Elmer, dislocated from his family's land, adopts a fatalistic lifestyle, understanding that he can never again return home. Finally, Jaxie's successful winning streak outside of the South brings him closer to his Georgia roots. Like the Old Testament God, the South that Starnes depicts can be rough and violent, but like God of the New Testament, it will welcome you home if you know how to find it.

Works Cited

Starnes, Joe Samuel. *Calling*. Lookout Mountain, TN: Jefferson Press, 2005.

Starnes, Joe Samuel. *Fall Line*. Montgomery, AL: NewSouth Books, 2011.

Starnes, Joe Samuel. "Larry Brown: A Firefighter Finds His Voice." In *Rough South, Rural South: Region and Class in Recent Southern Literature*, edited by Jean W. Cash and Keith Perry, 50–58. Jackson: University Press of Mississippi, 2016.

Starnes, Joe Samuel. "Larry Brown: Mentor from Afar." *Yalobusha Review: Literary Journal of the University of Mississippi* 6 (2006): 13–16.

Starnes, Joe Samuel. *Red Dirt*. Halcottsville, NY: Breakaway Books, 2015.

Jamie Quatro is the author of *I Want to Show You More* (2013), a story collection; and *Fire Sermon* (2018), a novel. She has received fellowships from Yaddo, MacDowell, Sewanee, and Bread Loaf. A contributing editor at *Oxford American*, she holds graduate degrees from Bennington College and the College of William and Mary. Her work has appeared in *Tin House*, the *Kenyon Review*, *AGNI*, and *Virginia Quarterly Review*. She has also received a Pushcart Prize. She lives with her husband and children in Lookout Mountain, Georgia.

Of All Things Sacred and Sensual
The Fiction of Jamie Quatro

Nick Ripatrazone

In a review of *I Want to Show You More*, Jamie Quatro's debut collection of stories, the critic James Wood praised Quatro's women: they "yearn and lust" with "an exciting literary freedom." Yet their "infidelities and imagined infidelities play out against the shadow of Christian belief and Christian prohibition. This is unusual, not just in contemporary fiction but perhaps in modern fiction generally" (Wood, "Broken Vows"). Wood is correct: such a tension is unmistakable, and rare. Contemporary American fiction is replete with women and men who yearn, lust, and more for a spiritual reality but do so against a secular backdrop. Quatro's characters are sincere in their usage of the word *sin*. They are often Christian, usually evangelical (sometimes vaguely fundamentalist). Fantasies—sensual, sexual, and more—charge them. In Quatro's fiction, however, when characters behave badly, they are aware of it.

Why, then, is this theme rare in contemporary American fiction? Sincere religious belief in fiction feels like an artifact of the 1960s—a decade when Walker Percy and J. F. Powers both won National Book Awards for novels about characters who were earnest about their religious searches, and when Flannery O'Connor was telling God-haunted yarns. Now, save for a handful of literary writers like Joy Williams, fiction about God usually appears in the ironic mode. God is not fully absent from contemporary American fiction, but God is artifice. Religious belief appears in a nostalgic sense, as a relic of youth.

Like Williams—and, in a particular sense, like O'Connor and Cormac McCarthy before her—Quatro imbues her fiction with a southern sense of religious strangeness. The piety of her characters is always a little off-center. Even Andre Dubus, another Christian writer from the South, operated on a different, more plainly domestic mode. The sins of his characters felt more prosaic; Quatro, in contrast, opens the door to signs and wonders of a more eschatological variety.

I Want to Show You More begins with a vision. "It was always the same," the narrator of "Caught Up" says of her childhood experiences (1). Back then, alone on her front patio, she watched "thick clouds above the mountains turn shades of red and purple, then draw themselves together and spiral" (1). Wind slapped hair against her face. "Then came a tugging in my middle, as if I were a kite about to be yanked up by a string attached just below my navel" (1). She felt that if she gave into that tug, she could "be catapulted, belly-first, into the vortex" (1). But her vision always ended there. She "never left the patio" (1). It is a fitting introduction for a sequence of stories where characters want more—want to show more—but often do not. Now older, the narrator no longer has those types of visions. She is married, but she has fallen in love with a man "who lives nine hundred miles away" (2). Their daily phone conversations have evolved into a planned meeting. The narrator tells her mother of this plan and is rebuked. She must have known such a response was coming; years earlier, when she'd told her mother of her childhood visions, her mother "said we should always be ready for the Lord's return: lead a clean life and stay busy with our work, keeping an eye skyward" (1). Now her mother's response is terse: forget this man.

She can't. He speaks to her in language that is as much sexual as it is sacred: "It would be devotional," he says of their love (2). "I would lay myself on your tongue like a Communion wafer" (2). The narrator swoons at these words, for they are a play on the religious language of her youth—a religious language that is patently corporal. Here Quatro's religious sincerity is essential. For an ironic writer, or one for whom religion is mere artifice and entertainment, this appropriation would feel trite. Instead, this is the only language that Quatro's characters know. God is within them and around them, and when lust and love blur, so do the parameters of religious language. The would-be lovers never meet. The narrator's reasons are a mixture of nerves and guilt; however, years later, she confesses to her mother how much she misses the man. Expecting some measure of understanding, she receives none. "You might as well have," her mother says of the canceled meetup (4). "It's all the same in God's eyes" (4).

"Caught Up" begins a series of stories in *I Want to Show You More* that put such ideas to the test. In "What Friends Talk About," the main character takes her children to school and then drives to a grocery, where she sits on a covered balcony. "This is where she goes to call the other man, though some days he calls her first" (59). The narrator makes this pronouncement gently, casually, in the second sentence of the story.

In Quatro's fiction, women are unhappy in their marriages, but not necessarily because of their husbands. Often those men are kind, doting, and devoted. They are never cruel; however, emotionally and sexually, they are not what these women need—or have grown to need. That need soon becomes all-consuming for Quatro's characters. In "What Friends Talk About," the woman makes constant "lists of things she wants to ask or tell the other man" (59). She fills receipts and the insides of book covers. She talks about her husband and her daughter.

The "other man" is, after all, a friend first. A companion. That's how she feels, at least; he prefers to avoid speaking about their domestic lives and commitments. He changes the subject. They talk about poetry, reading passages aloud. They record themselves reading verses (orality is essential to Quatro's idea of seduction). They speak of quantum physics, spirituality, and even C. S. Lewis and the Psalms—every subject a flirtation in its own way.

Quatro's pacing and style are masterful on these points. As a writer of passion, she is without contemporary equal, her writing perfectly attuned to the desires of her characters. In "What Friends Talk About," the phone conversations are not delivered as direct dialogue but offered secondhand. The result is that they are far more intimate. The woman calls their affair an "addiction," and it is (61). She longs for his calls. She even plans her daughter's piano lessons as an "hour of near-privacy" in which she can speak with the man (65). We know these actions are foolish. They also feel downright immoral; and here Quatro's skill lies in making us arrive at such a conclusion, and not quite from a place of judgment. By creating a world in which sin is real, and constant, and yet still morally *wrong*, Quatro allows us to watch characters bend the rules they have created for their lives, without necessarily repenting. Once again, the story ends with the lovers apart, never having physically met. This repetition creates a powerful tension in Quatro's work. Her characters are fully aware of the desires and needs of their bodies, but communication and consummation occur at a physical distance, remaining deeply internal, in their minds. Sex remains often fully in the realm of fantasy, any physical connection staying there, but still palpable.

The most physical moments of *I Want to Show You More* arrive in Quatro's description of running. A runner herself, she authentically captures the exhausting, even rapturous feeling of the sport. In the story "Ladies and Gentleman of the Pavement," runners are a practical bunch, with "a unique economy surrounding bodily functions. With a finger we close one nostril and blow snot from the other—without breaking pace—to avoid carrying tissues" (23). She channels their movement: "Breathing, coughing, hacking, and spitting. The thumping of shoes on pavement. Above these sounds, birdsong" (28).

Running in Quatro's fiction acquires nearly the same significance as the sexual longing of her characters. When she writes of the misconceptions of "runner's high," she seems metaphorically attuned to the evolution of desire (31). This high is not "a sudden leap into euphoria" (31). Instead it is "a gradual transition into a state of mental clarity. . . . The smallest details become sharp. My senses open up and I can take everything in—telephone wires silhouetted against blue sky, layered bark on the trunk of a tree" (31). Later her body dissipates. She doesn't feel her feet touch the ground. That "separation of mind from flesh, spirit from matter, is what keeps me coming back for more" (32).

Could we call such moments religious visions? Quatro opens that door. As she moves further in her collection, Quatro's stories feel even more suffused with a religious sense. In "The Anointing," Diane wants to have the church elders anoint her husband with oil: "Anointings were eleventh-hour efforts— what you asked for after you'd asked for everything else" (86). A doctor, he has been addicted to Vicodin for years and was fined by the DEA. Her faith "waning," Diane doubts the anointing will work, but she has no other choice (88). When the pastor arrives, "carrying a family-sized bottle of Wesson Oil," we feel the absurdity of hope (90).

"Demolition," a finely tuned story delivered in numbered, often prose-poetic sections, feels like the apex of Quatro's development in the collection. A series of strange events, starting in Lent, befall a small church. A deaf man and a boy, his interpreter, arrive at the service. During the sermon, the "boy mimic[s] the snap of scissors across his uplifted forearm for *shepherd*, for *sorrow* stroke[s] the air with fluttering fingers as if brushing aside a beaded curtain" (160). He seems as if he comes from a charismatic denomination.

The parishioners are hypnotized by him, and they are compelled by his dual devotion: to God, and to the man. Around that time, Christ's foot falls from a stained glass window—during Communion no less. The mysterious man stands and, through his interpreter, confesses his unbelief. Over time, the oddities continue: more broken glass, parishioners fleeing for other churches, and, finally, the decision to demolish the church. In the midst of this destruction, the mysterious man returns as a prophet, delivering heresy: "We can enter eternity here, on this planet" (175).

The man convinces the remaining congregation to cast aside shame and to confess their greatest sins to the group. A church without a building, they have flocked to a cave and a clearing, where the story descends into cultic reverie—a scene that would make O'Connor's characters blush. Their children hide in the woods: "Sometimes we glimpsed them in the trees, peering down at us, hanging loose, obscuring their faces" (181). Soon one of the members of the group is dead, and their leader vanishes.

By the end of "Demolition," Quatro has conjured a mystical horror story about a group consumed by the presence of signs and wonders while forgetting about love. Dizzy and drunk with their closeness to one another, the group members watch their children build their own community—convinced they will come back to them. It is an eerie conclusion to a wild tale told with frightening detail and care. The work begs to be followed by more stories that teeter on the edges of horror, sexuality, and religion.

Fire Sermon, Quatro's debut novel, takes the best elements of her story collection—unabashed strangeness, eschatology channeled down into domestic spaces, characters drunk with desire and delusion, and theologically rich prose—and wraps them in an epistolary narrative. Maggie and James are both forty-five years old, both married for over twenty years to their spouses. Both born and raised in the Southwest, they are "students of the Christian mystics and quantum theory and *Moby Dick*" (*Fire Sermon*, 12).

The novel arrives in bated journal entries and letters, the genres blurring at certain moments. Maggie and James are in love and in lust, wholly consumed by the melodrama of their affair. "Foolish," Maggie writes, "the way lovers scaffold passion with symbology, constructing a joint past which seems, even after a few hours, immemorial" (21). Some reviewers of *Fire Sermon* were turned off by Maggie's effusiveness, the novel's pulpy moments—there are, to be sure, times when the writing pushes up against erotic pastiche—but such criticisms miss the point. *Fire Sermon* is a book lodged deep in the psyches of characters who have lost their moral way. As Maggie says, they have not only fallen in love with each other but also fallen in love with the rhetorical and even literary idea of an affair.

Like the husbands in *I Want to Show You More*, Maggie's spouse is no villain. He is "a good husband. He works long hours so she can stay in grad school full-time" (29). He cooks for her, goes to church with her, and reads drafts of her essays. Their sexual life is strained—to put it lightly. He is simply not what she wants, and what she needs, at this moment. Selfish? Possibly. Quatro's characters often don't make good decisions.

But they have the room to make those bad decisions—and that they do so within a Christian schema is doubly unique. Maggie writes journal entries to James, but she also writes to God. She asks for forgiveness. "I have this space in me," she laments, "and God is not there and emptiness is not there" (36). In unsent letters to James, she muses on their brief shared time together, when they both attended a literary conference. They speak of God and theology; she misses the "delight, the utter joy of speaking with someone who shared the language of my childhood" (44). They speak of the "ontological versus cosmological arguments for the existence of God, and whether the universe exists *in esse*, like a house (deism, Aristotle) or *in fieri*, liquid in a vessel (theism, Aquinas)" (44).

To read such discussion in a contemporary novel is not merely rare; it is confounding. Quatro's characters exist in a God-drenched world. Creed is less important than the all-pervading presence of the divine. God is everywhere. It is almost as if we are in a version of Flannery O'Connor's letters to Betty Hester—a theological dance. This dance intertwines memory, liturgy, sexuality, all tied within the same breaths of syntax. *Fire Sermon* is a song of despair. In much the same way as Quatro's characters are branded by the religious faith of their youth, once burned by attraction, they can never escape. As *Fire Sermon* accumulates, we feel breaths of previous novels in the mystical mode: think of Ron Hansen's *Mariette in Ecstasy* and Gustave Flaubert's *The Temptation of Saint Anthony*. Quatro's fiction suggests that the passion and power of religious language burst out of their original vessel. Her characters are so charged with belief—and its sister, doubt—that they can use only that vocabulary when describing any other emotion that pierces their souls. We should read Quatro as a literary descendant of O'Connor and other skilled writers of fiction haunted by religion, but she takes her own, fresh route: she is a writer who has made desire nearly devotional.

Works Cited

Quatro, Jamie. *Fire Sermon*. Grove Press, 2018.

Quatro, Jamie. *I Want to Show You More*. Grove Press, 2013.

Wood, James. "Broken Vows." *New Yorker*, March 11, 2013. https://www.newyorker.com/magazine /2013/03/11/broken-vows. Accessed August 8, 2018.

Michael Farris Smith was born and grew up in Mississippi, where his father was a Baptist minister. He graduated from Mississippi State University and afterward spent several years in Europe, working with an events company for the NBA. While there, he began to read modern American literature, the works of Hemingway, Fitzgerald, Faulkner, and O'Connor, among others. After returning to Oxford, Mississippi, he visited Square Books and discovered the fiction of Larry Brown and Barry Hannah. He later earned degrees from William Carey College in Hattiesburg, Mississippi, and a PhD from the University of Southern Mississippi; he taught for a number of years at the University of Mississippi for Women in Columbus. He now lives and writes in Oxford, Mississippi. He has published the novella *The Hands of Strangers* (2011) and the novels *Rivers* (2013), *Desperation Road* (2017), *The Fighter* (2018), *Blackwood* (2020), and *Nick* (2021). Among his awards are the Mississippi Arts Commission Literary Arts Fellowship, the Transatlantic Review Award for Fiction, the Alabama Arts Council Fellowship Award for Literature, and the Brick Streets Press Short Story Award. He has twice been nominated for a Pushcart Prize (for his stories) and has published essays in the *New York Times*, *Catfish Alley*, and elsewhere.

Michael Farris Smith
"Truckin' to Success"

Jean W. Cash

Of the more than twenty southern writers of fiction who began to publish after 2000, Michael Farris Smith has, by 2018, published more books than most and received global acclaim, even traveling to Adelaide, Australia, to promote *Desperation Road*. Critics and readers are enthusiastic about his work. In a review of Smith's novel *The Fighter*, *Kirkus Reviews* calls Smith "a gifted storyteller who parses battered dreams and the legacies of abandonment with a harsh realism that is both saddening and engaging." Emerging as a writer in the mode of Larry Brown, Smith depicts working-class people, revealing the grittiness of their lives, but like Brown, Smith is a genuine humanitarian who cares about the people he creates and stimulates the same positive response in readers. Reviewing *Desperation Road*, Jim Ewing suggests that Brown's down-and-out southerners depict the displaced working man in an increasingly mechanized society: "[We] now have a post-modern society with industrial outsourcing of jobs to foreign shores and its concomitant decline of American manufacturing, the imperative of higher education as the ticket for the now lottery for middle-class success, and the rise of two-earner families essential for economic survival that has added minorities and women to dilute white male hegemony." In his novels, Smith sympathetically treats his characters—not just the males—as "dislocated, lost, and perhaps even doomed" (Ewing, "*Desperation Road*").

44

Smith began to write the novella *The Hands of Strangers* while he was still in graduate school. He was publishing stories in local journals but had little luck getting his first full-length manuscript accepted for publication; it was a novella. He has said that he chose that form because "some of my favorite books are novellas, *The Stranger, The Old Man and the Sea, The Ballad of the Sad Cafe*. It's a wonderful form" ("Michael F. Smith on Writing").

His failure to get *The Hands of Strangers* published was like that of Larry Brown in the years before he had any stories published. Editors told both writers that their works were worthy of publication but not suitable for their press or magazines. Smith, like Brown, refused to give up, continuing to write. After the natural horrors brought on by Hurricane Katrina, Smith began his novel *Rivers*. When it was half finished and Smith was on the verge of giving up writing—by then he was teaching at the Mississippi University for Women in Columbus—his novella was accepted, and his career as a writer launched.

The Hands of Strangers is his only book not set in Mississippi; even though it takes place in Paris, his main character is an expatriate southerner not too different from William Styron's central character in *Set This House on Fire*. Both protagonists hold on to southern values—particularly that of family—in an environment far different from where they grew up. In an early interview, Smith gives background to the story:

> The inspiration came from a strange, sad moment. I was in the Paris metro and in some of the bigger metro halls, there are public boards where people put up flyers for concerts, new stores, bars, and so on. As I was walking past one of these, I saw a homemade flyer that said, "Please help us find our daughter," and it included a black and white photo of a young girl. It stopped me and really struck me in an emotional way. Days went by and I couldn't stop thinking about it, so I sat down and wrote a short story titled "Anywhere" that was my imagining the father, walking through these metro halls, with a duffel bag full of these flyers. I just went on from there. ("Michael F. Smith on Writing")

Written in the clear and vivid diction that has characterized all his fiction, the story explores what happens to parents whose nine-year-old daughter mysteriously disappears while on a school field trip. His believable depiction of the psychological trauma that each parent experiences helps create a griping story of suspense, one strongly realistic without melodrama until the end when the girl reappears, having been kidnapped by a group of villains who steal children to sell, not into the sex trade but to parents who are dissatisfied with the children they already have.

By the time *The Hands of Strangers* came out in 2011, Smith was well into *Rivers*. Living in Alabama at the time of the hurricane, he did not directly experience Katrina but had relatives who were living in southern Mississippi during the storm. In a radio interview in March 2013, Smith said:

> For a couple of years, I wanted to write a post-Katrina novel, but I kept starting and stopping and it wasn't working. . . . I didn't like fabricating . . . that heartbreak. . . . I kept thinking about it and I don't know why I thought of it this way, but one day I just imagined, "What if we just jacked Katrina up about fifty times over and what if for a couple or even five or even six or seven or eight years the Gulf coast was just one Katrina after another?" ("Dialogue")

Rivers is clearly an apocalyptic novel, one in some ways superior to Cormac McCarthy's *The Road* (2006). Unlike McCarthy, Smith makes clear the cause of Gulf Coast ruin: post-Katrina changes in weather and climate patterns. Smith's characterization is also superior to McCarthy's. While McCarthy's work is clearly allegorical, Smith's is realistic. His people face and suffer the kind of natural horror that most of us can only imagine. His central character, Cohen, is the prototype of the strong American individualist.

After the government establishes the Line, an arbitrary barrier beyond which nobody can legally live, Cohen realizes that staying below the Line will be futile. But, bound by loyalty to his dead wife and child, he refuses to leave his home, where his southern family has lived for generations. Smith's novel, of necessity, features high melodrama, but it transcends the melodrama through its believability. The people who remain in the area are simple victims with no means of escape, stubbornly individualistic like Cohen, or power hungry and evil like the maniacal Aggie, a would-be despot who seeks to create his own oligarchy. Despite Aggie's evil nature, however, Smith is able to give him a modicum of humanity.

In FEMA trailers left over from Katrina, Aggie sets up a miniature community with female survivors of the deluge. He and his sidekick set out to impregnate the women, seeking to build their private anti-utopia. Besides Aggie's monomania, Smith also introduces American greed as a theme of his tale. Characters like Charlie look to make a killing by selling black-market goods to the hapless survivors. Charlie and some of these people—and others who have deliberately sneaked into the area—seek buried treasure, money stashed, they think, by the owners of the ruined Gulf Coast casinos. The most compelling part of the novel, however, involves Cohen's rescue of three young people who have unwittingly become part of Aggie's tribe: two brothers, Evan and Brisco, and a young woman, Mariposa, from New Orleans. In *Rivers*, Smith creates a novel both dramatic and touching, one that deals with human disaster and degradation, the human need for connection, and the possibility for rejuvenation, even under the most horrific circumstances.

Smith published his second full-length novel, *Desperation Road*, in early 2017. This novel works as the ultimate tribute to Larry Brown. Smith builds on two of Brown's most significant characters, Glenn Davis from *Father and Son* and Fay Jones from *Fay*. Russell, in Smith's novel, is an almost obverse reflection of Glenn Davis. Both men have served time for vehicular homicide, but their earlier backgrounds and future behaviors could not be more different. Psychologically stunted since his youth by parents who never should have married, Glenn Davis seems doomed to an early death. His time in prison has left him even more emotionally fragile than when he entered, and has triggered in him an irrational need for revenge. Drunk, he had run down a child but accepts no personal responsibility. Russell, on the other hand, drunk too, killed a young man but realizes his culpability. Traumatized by his time in Parchman, Russell returns from prison still hoping to make a better life. He knows that he can never rekindle his relationship with his now-married former fiancée, but he still has personal fortitude and a supportive father who will do anything to aid his son's redemption. Besides trying to reclaim his reputation as a decent human being, from the day of his release, Russell must deal with the vengeful brothers of the boy he killed.

Smith's Maben is a grown-up Fay: she has spent many years on the road that Fay has just begun to travel, but Maben's outcome is clearly pitiable. That Smith brings Russell and Maben together through the irony of circumstance shows how little control we ultimately have over our existence. In some ways, Brown's *Father and Son* is a study of the psychological ruin of one man and the damage he can do to those around him, whereas *Desperation Road* is a story of redemption, or at least the attempt to achieve it. Though the novel's plot is somewhat convoluted as Smith uses coincidence to brings his co-protagonists together, his characters are fully and realistically conceived; his treatment of Maben and her child is particularly poignant, and his inclusion of the revenge-seeking brothers introduces evil in its most brutal form. His handling of Russell's father, Mitchell, is much different from Brown's treatment of Virgil in *Father and* Son, but both men seem real despite their respective losses.

Smith's second novel received numerous positive reviews that helped to move him ahead as a serious writer. Joe Hartlaub, wondering how Smith would follow up his success with *Rivers*, writes, "*Desperation Road* doesn't meet or exceed expectation so much as blows the doors, windows, and roofs off of the house in which it lives. It's a book for which you'll want to set aside everything else." Several reviewers praise Smith's skill with language, including Jim Ewing: "The book is elegant, even profound, the cadence of the words alluring, bringing the reader deeper into . . . [his] world of gray." The *Kirkus* reviewer, describing Smith's prose as "shapely" and his dialogue as "sharp," goes on to applaud his "acute sense of the moments and pain that can define lives in a small town." The novel was an Amazon Best Book of the Month, an Indie Next Pick, a Barnes & Noble Discover Pick, and one of *Southern Living*'s Best Southern Books of 2017. Most recently Smith has announced that both *Desperation Road* and *The Fighter* are under serious consideration by Hollywood filmmakers.

Little, Brown and Company published Smith's third novel, *The Fighter*, in March 2018. Jack Boucher, the title character, emerges as Smith's most fully realized character to date. Smith depicts this tragically wounded man in terms that evoke considerable empathy. Smith has described his original conception of the character:

> All my novels have started with some really strong image that I just can't shake and for me, it was Jack Boucher, his physical and mental pain and anguish. . . . How would he cope with it and deal with it?—and I just went right to the painkillers. If he has fought like this for 20 years, then he has certainly suffered brain damage, and chunks of his memory would certainly be beginning to fade away. The extremity of his situation came alive for me very quickly. (Smith, "Michael Farris Smith: Author of The Fighter")

Abandoned by his parents when he was only two years old, Jack becomes a victim of the welfare system until at the age of twelve he is taken in by Maryann, a lonely single woman, the last remnant of a Deep South family. She knows that she is a lesbian, but family pride, love for her ancestral home, and existential despair leave her unable to accept herself as she is. She withdraws into a cocoon of loneliness until she takes in the needy boy. Both draw strength from that connection. Smith has said of their relationship, "I think the relationship between Jack and Maryann is the most tender relationship I've written in my novels. I came upon emotions while writing the novel that I was really surprised by. My first instinct was to back away. But then I just really wanted to embrace it. There is something of a miracle for both Jack and her in that relationship" ("Michael Farris Smith: A Novel like a Bullet Train").

To Jack she becomes the mother that he never had; his devotion to her continues throughout his life as a cage fighter. He seems to have chosen to become a fighter out of some psychological need to fight a world that, even with Maryann's loving concern, he never understands. As he launches into his last cage battle,

> he searched for every fragment of hate and resentment and the fragments came with sharp edges. He found the rughaired boy and the blank faces of a woman and man who emptied him into this world and he found the anxiety of abandonment and the black hours of childhood loneliness and desolation of the unknown. He found fanged faces of addiction that had lived with him in the musty rooms and he found the long and lasting losing streaks where he flushed away the work of generations for the sake of simple selfish thrills. (236)

Accepting the horror of his own selfish blindness, Jack launches into this last battle. Smith leaves the end partly open: he wins the fight, but whether he survives it is uncertain. No happy endings here.

In structuring the novel, Smith uses both a prologue and epilogue with a three-part inner structure that he calls "Round One," "Round Two," and "Round Three," suggesting, as the *Kirkus* reviewer writes, that Smith "could be nodding to the classical unities of place and time, with his three-day plot centered on Clarksdale, Mississippi." To introduce the past history of Jack, Maryann, and Annette, Smith uses flashbacks that effectively provide essential background on the often sad history of all three characters. His use of the letters Maryann kept from her early relationship also add depth to our understanding of this complex woman; they are also important to Jack's realizations of what she has given up for him.

Smith also introduces subplots, one centering on a tawdry carnival operation reminiscent of those that still move through the South. The second is that of Big Mama Sweet, whom Emily Choate describes as hanging "over the novel as Jack's greatest nemesis. To owe her money is to watch your life's clock running down fast." With the carnival group, Brown introduces secondary characters: Baron, the manager, who gets involved in Jack's life by being there at a pivotal moment. A more interesting member of the carnival crew is Annette, a young woman as lost as Jack who has tried to give her life meaning with multiple tattoos, a bit reminiscent of Flannery O'Connor's O. E. Parker. Choate suggests that "these supporting characters form a kind of archetypal backdrop for Jack, whose depth and humanity provide the true engine for 'The Fighter.'"

Smith's use of coincidence—first important in *Desolation Road*—hovers over this novel as well. Allen Mudge believes Annette uses the "church of coincidence in her own theology to help herself believe that there is an answer for her somewhere" (Smith, "Michael Farris Smith: A Novel"). Jack and the Outlaw Carnival coincidentally come together, just as Jack and Annette do after she has left the carnival with Jack's money that he so desperately needs. Coincidentally, she may also be his daughter. Smith repeats several motifs through the novel: the brass knuckles so important in Jack's final battle appear several times. The hawk as a being free from human troubles appears intermittently, and most significantly, the angelic appearance of a mysterious figure (perhaps Maryann?) adds a quasi-mystical element to the novel early and again at the end.

Overall, *The Fighter* is a strong novel that received a good deal of positive comment by early reviewers. Smith's characterization of Jack Boucher is complete and remarkable, and as one reviewer asserts:

> Smith writes about desperation and last chances more effectively than most authors out there. The Fighter is often brutal and relentless, but there are notes of hope. Jack is a fascinating character, and you are drawn into his struggles, even if you have a feeling you know where things will end up. The story of his hard-fought childhood and the woman who saved him is poignant, and you understand why he's willing to risk everything for her. ("Book Review: 'The Fighter'")

In 2018, Smith published a short essay, "Keep Truckin'," in *Southern Writers on Writing*, edited by Susan Cushman. He tells how he chose to become a writer, his difficulties in getting published, and his constant dedication to his craft. At the end, he says, "I see the pieces of my writing life fitting together. I couldn't see it then. No one can. And through all the rejection and frustration, one thing remained constant. I kept writing. I kept working. There is no substitute. You have to do the work and believe in yourself when no one else does" (186).

In May 2018, Smith announced the publication of his next novel, scheduled for release in 2019. A preannouncement from Little, Brown describes the novel, titled *Blackwood*, as "a haunted tale rising out of a vine-covered valley, where a woman and twin boys have gone missing, and a man with his own twisted past struggles to untangle their shocking disappearances, while a trio of mysterious vagabonds linger on the outskirts of a Mississippi where ghostly whispers fill the night." As advertised, this new novel contains elements from *Desperation Road* and *The Fighter* with waves to both Larry Brown and Cormac McCarthy.

The migrant family at the outset of the novel resembles the Jones family in two of Larry Brown's novels, *Joe* and *Fay.* To Brown's portrayal, however, Smith adds even more hopelessness, as well as a sort of maniacal evil to the ungainly patriarch of the family and greater horror for the son. In this "trio of mysterious vagabonds," Smith somewhat reflects Cormac McCarthy's triune in *Outer Dark.* Colburn, the novel's central character, also seems to reflect McCarthy's treatment of the seventy-eight-year-old Billy Parham at the end of *Cities of the Plain.*

Throughout the novel, Colburn resembles Cohen in Smith's *Rivers* in his artistic sensitivity and his inability to establish a strong sense of identity. Haunted by the death of a younger sibling and his role in his father's suicide, Colburn has become a wanderer and a would-be artist who seems doomed to failure. A youngish man at the beginning of the story, he has drifted through his life, never forming a successful relationship with anyone. New elements in the novel include a cave perhaps reminiscent of Poe's in "The Pit and Pendulum"; however, Smith's treatment of landscape in the new novel continues to emphasize both its beauty and its mysterious power. Enthusiasts of Smith's work should look forward to this new book; it shows Smith's continued interest in the southern underclass, the quest for meaning in life, and his continued commanding power of language.

Works Cited

Announcement for *Blackwood*. Facebook, May 10, 2018.

"Book Review: 'The Fighter' by Michael Farris Smith." *It's Either Sadness or Bookphoria,* February 15, 2018. https://itseithersadnessoreuphoria.blogspot.com/2018/02/book-review -fighter-by-michael-farris.html. Accessed September 10, 2018.

52Jean W. Cash

Cash, Jean W. "Twenty-First Century Writers: The Rural Southern Tradition Continues." In
Rough South, Rural South: Region and Class in Recent Southern Literature, edited by Jean
W. Cash and Keith Perry, 210–23. University Press of Mississippi, 2016.
Choate, Emily. "Michael Farris Smith's Protagonist in 'The Fighter' Is Shattered but Persistent."
Knoxville News Sentinel, April 14, 2018. https://www.knoxnews.com/story/life/2018/04/14
/michael-farris-smith-fighter-book-review-protagonist-shattered-but-persistent/506705002.
Accessed September 10, 2018.
"Desperation Road, by Michael Farris Smith." Kirkus Reviews, February 7, 2017. https://www
.kirkusreviews.com/book-reviews/michael-farris-smith/desperation-road. Accessed
September 10, 2018.
Ewing, Jim. "Desperation Road." Jackson Clarion-Ledger, January 29, 2017. https://www.clarion
ledger.com/story/magnolia/books/2017/01/29/book-review-desperation-road-michael
-farris-smith-jim-ewing/96629184. Accessed September 10, 2018.
"The Fighter, by Michael Farris Smith." Kirkus Reviews, March 20, 2018. https://www.kirkus
reviews.com/book-reviews/michael-farris-smith/the-fighter-smith. Accessed September
10, 2018.
Hartlaub, Joe. "Review: Desperation Road by Michael Farris Smith." Bookreporter, February 24,
2017. https://www.bookreporter.com/reviews/desperation-road. Accessed September 10,
2018.
Hoops, Jana. "Author Q&A: Michael Farris Smith." Jackson Clarion-Ledger, February 5, 2017.
https://www.clarionledger.com/story/magnolia/books/2017/02/05/author-interview
-michael-farris-smith-jana-hoops/96629110. Accessed September 10, 2018.
Smith, Michael Farris. Desperation Road. Little, Brown, 2017.
Smith, Michael Farris. "Dialogue." Real Media, March 28, 2013. https://www.thisrealmedia.com.
Smith, Michael Farris. The Fighter. Little, Brown, 2018.
Smith, Michael Farris. The Hands of Strangers. Main Street Rag Publishing, 2011.
Smith, Michael Farris. "Keep Truckin'." In Southern Writers on Writing, edited by Susan
Cushman, 183–86. University Press of Mississippi, 2018.
Smith, Michael Farris. "Michael F. Smith on Writing, Paris and His Debut Novel, The Hands
of Strangers." Interview with Emerald Barnes. Dreaming Awake, July 21, 2011. https://
ebarnes23.wordpress.com/2011/07/19/michael-f-smith-on-writing-paris-and-his-debut
-novella-the-hands-of-strangers. Accessed September 10, 2018.
Smith, Michael Farris. "Michael Farris Smith: A Novel like a Bullet Train." Interview with
Alden Mudge. BookPage, April 2018. https://bookpage.com/interviews/22516-michael
-farris-smith#.WwROsCZdP6U. Accessed September 10, 2018.
Smith, Michael Farris. "Michael Farris Smith: Author of The Fighter." Interview with Megan
Labrise. Kirkus Reviews, March 22, 2018. https://www.kirkusreviews.com/features/michael
-farris-smith. Accessed September 10, 2018.
Smith, Michael Farris. Rivers. Simon & Schuster, 2013.
Swoope, Jan. "Launch for Smith's Debut Novella Set for Thursday." Columbus and Starkville
Dispatch, April 11, 2011. https://www.cdispatch.com. Accessed April 12, 2011.

Tayari Jones is the author of the novels *Leaving Atlanta*, *The Untelling*, *Silver Sparrow*, and *An American Marriage*. Her writing has appeared in *Tin House*, *The Believer*, the *New York Times*, and *Callaloo*. A member of the Fellowship of Southern Writers, she has also been a recipient of the Hurston/Wright Legacy Award, Lifetime Achievement Award in Fine Arts from the Congressional Black Caucus Foundation, United States Artist Fellowship, NEA Fellowship, and Radcliffe Institute Bunting Fellowship. *Silver Sparrow* was added to the NEA Big Read library of classics in 2016. Jones is a graduate of Spelman College, University of Iowa, and Arizona State University. She is a professor of creative writing at Emory University.

Difficult Women

Tayari Jones and the
Recuperation of Representations

Destiny O. Birdsong

The famed comedian Chris Rock once said that Major League Baseball was not truly integrated until the 1970s, when mediocre players began getting major deals. "True equality is the equality to suck like the white man," says Rock. "I want to be like that. Not that I want to be bad, but I want . . . the license to be bad, and come back, and learn." While I would never use the term "mediocrity" to describe Tayari Jones's canon—her ability to write about the Black South, its inhabitants, and the ways in which race, place, and class impact multiple generations of family members places her in a league of her own—such could certainly be said about her young Black women narrators. By their own admission, they are not overtly beautiful: Ariadne "Aria" Jackson, the protagonist of Jones's 2005 novel, *The Untelling*, describes her looks as "plain as paper" (114), and Octavia Fuller, one of the fifth-grade narrators from *Leaving Atlanta* (2002), describes her blackness as one that "don't quite lay right" compared to her equally dark-skinned and beautiful father and half sister (208). Jones's women are also not particularly moral in the traditional sense: Aria conceals her infertility to keep a shotgun marriage proposal from her short-term boyfriend, Dwayne, whom she has erroneously told she is pregnant, and Celestial Davenport Hamilton ultimately leaves her wrongfully incarcerated husband, Roy, for their mutual friend, Andre. Jones's women fail in devastating, but unintentional and ordinary, ways, and they fail at relationships, at honesty, and even, in some cases, at motherhood. This is a far cry from their literary ancestors, slave narrators like Harriet Jacobs's Linda Brent, who implores the reader to forgive her romantic relationship with Mr. Sands, a white man whom she never marries, but who fathers both of her children; or even Toni Morrison's Sula, who destroys her loved ones' lives out of a general sense of privilege and mild amusement. On the contrary, the women of Tayari Jones's canon are neither villainously bad nor unwaveringly good; they are not martyrs for the race, nor are they traitors to any kind of ideal. This is perhaps one of her most profound contributions to contemporary Black southern literature: Black women characters who reserve the right to be human, and flawed, and struggle to learn from those flaws before the reader's very eyes. By doing so, they do far more than push back against what Patricia Hill Collins calls the four tropes of Black womanhood: the mammies, matriarchs, Sapphires, and Jezebels that have plagued representation for centuries.[1] Instead these women live, love, and lie as if those restrictive categories, and the white gaze that has long held these tropes in place, never existed.

One of Jones's greatest feats as an author is her ability to write from multiple perspectives, from prepubescent girls inhabiting the rough neighborhoods of 1970s Atlanta, to well-to-do, college-educated artists of the present day, and everything in between. Her first novel, *Leaving Atlanta* (2002), is told in the voices of three different characters: LaTasha Baxter, whose staunchly middle-class household is nearly torn apart by divorce, until the onset of missing Black children from nearby neighborhoods frightens her father back home; Rodney Green, Tasha's classmate and an intelligent (albeit unmotivated) boy whose discontent with his father drives him into a killer's arms; and Octavia Fuller, the daughter of a single mother who is struggling to make good on her promise to get out of Macon and make something of herself in a city that has little regard for the welfare and safety of her growing daughter. Perhaps the most nuanced (and, I would argue, the most interesting) voice in the text is Octavia's, because despite her age and her lack of the privilege of LaTasha and Rodney, whose Black parents enjoy relative success in this progressive southern city, Octavia is a keen observer of her world and the people in it. Also, it is through her that we are introduced to a narrator and her mother, both of whom break several stereotypical character molds.

We are initially introduced to Octavia through LaTasha's narrative, when we learn that she is an outcast among her classmates, who call her Watusi—a playground epithet for "African" because of her dark skin. Like many of the children at her school, she lives nearby, in a rundown apartment building that is, as both she and her mother insist, not the projects, but just barely. Rumors spread that she has poor hygiene, and the rumors are so rampant that Tasha is surprised when, during a close encounter with Octavia, Tash discovers that Octavia "smell[s] like lemonade" (49). Octavia often sits and plays alone, but she is not without resources or, as we discover in later chapters, love.

First, Octavia is remarkably capable of standing up for herself. She does not shrink into a defenseless shell like most bullied children. She can hurl insults as deftly as she hurls rocks. When two older children imply that she and Rodney "like" each other because they are talking at recess, Octavia explodes. "You better shut your mouth, ol' ugly boy," snaps Octavia, who furiously begins throwing pebbles, hoping to make contact with her accusers (98). When one of them begins to ridicule her for her color, she counters, "Your hair is so nappy that the BB shots in the back look like you screwed them in one at a time" (99). Later she becomes angry at Rodney for denying a relationship between them to a cafeteria full of classmates who burst into laughter, and when he proffers a peace offering of pilfered corner store candy, she responds by sweeping it angrily onto the floor (101). And although Octavia is certainly friendly, she does not crumble when her overtures are rejected. When Tasha is spurned by her classmates for speaking brashly to a potential crush but balks when Octavia offers her space at her lonely table, Octavia is not bothered: "You don't have to sit here," she tells Tasha. "I was just trying to be nice" (48).

Second, despite even her own admission that she is not conventionally beautiful, Octavia is desirable (at least by elementary school definitions of the term): Rodney, who sits behind her in class, is both bewildered and intrigued by her moxie, her intelligence, and her kindness. When Rodney must help his father repair a leaky pipe in their front yard, Rodney wonders if this is a kidnapper's ploy to lure him outdoors. In response, he leaves a note in his bedroom divulging his whereabouts and prints Octavia's name on it, almost as if the note is addressed specifically to her. Later, just hours before he decides to get in the car of the man who will kill him, he tries to explain to her why his father has beaten him in front of the entire class, but like everyone else, she has trouble understanding him, and this final slight sends him into a tailspin of despair.

What I find most powerful about Octavia's character is that she is no shrinking dark violet, nor have her unfortunate home and school situations made her monstrous. She is both sassy and kind, quiet but keenly observant. She begins her narrative with a declaration, "My mother tells lies," and she lists several examples (143). Yvonne Fuller lies about everything from her brother's drug addiction to Octavia's safety when Yvonne's mother calls, alarmed by the news of disappearing children. Octavia also loves her mother deeply, but she does not offer her an easy out when Yvonne decides that Octavia might be safer with her father in South Carolina. While her mother tries to romanticize her departure with a fancy dress, perfume, and the insistence that she loves her, Octavia wants most for things to play out as they have been planned: "Taxi be here in a minute," she replies drily when her mother holds her too long in an embrace (254). But later Octavia ends her narrative and the book with the declaration "I'll be missing my mama for the rest of my life" (255). Indeed, despite her mother's flaws, and Octavia's own inability to understand the rationale for being sent away, Octavia finds room for devotion, loyalty, and deep love.

In fact, many of the nuances of Black women's characterization in Jones's work manifest themselves in the context of mother-daughter relationships, which are the hallmark of her third book, *Silver Sparrow* (2011), whose narrative is equally split between two sisters: Dana Lynn Yarboro and Bunny Chaurisse Witherspoon. Dana and Bunny are unwitting sisters/daughters to a man living a double life, and each woman's relationship with her mother shapes how she comes to terms with the revelation thereof. Dana's mother, Gwendolyn, is the second wife of James Witherspoon, owner of a private car company who has built a comfortable life for himself and his first family, Chaurisse and her mother, Laverne. Although Gwendolyn Yarboro knowingly became James's second wife, she is deeply embittered by her position. She often takes Dana on excursions to stake out the family, and she tries to mitigate Dana's burgeoning knowledge about her illegitimacy with comparisons between Dana and James's younger daughter, Chaurisse. "Look at her," Gwendolyn scoffs. "She hardly has any hair. She is going to be fat when she grows up, just like her mammy. She doesn't know her –*at* words, and she can't sing a song in French" (14). Indeed, unlike some of Jones's other protagonists, Dana is considered beautiful by those around her, but as the novel unfolds, the reader learns that that beauty is only skin deep; instead readers are naturally drawn to Chaurisse, who is openly insecure, compassionate, but also forthcoming about her feelings for her parents in her narrative, much like her own mother, Laverne (Fisher, "Daughters Get Their Day," 12).

Dana, on the contrary, becomes dangerously invested in her own beauty, which is the one asset she thinks she has over Chaurisse, who lives comfortably in a two-parent home and is not forced to attend schools and extracurricular events based on James's need to maintain secrecy. As Dana matures, she, like her mother, grows increasingly bitter, and she ultimately orchestrates Laverne's discovery of her existence when she stalks and pretends to befriend Chaurisse. By the end of the novel, Dana is a mother herself, but she seems somewhat fearful of what she knows from experience she can pass down to her own child, saying, "In so many ways, you can't choose what you give to your daughter, you just give her what you have" (335). And, true enough, Dana is very much her mother's daughter: when Chaurisse meets her in the parking lot of her daughter's school, Dana remarks that Chaurisse is wearing a man's suit and "look[s] like her mother [Laverne] from her dull figure to the silly mop of fake hair" (336). After Chaurisse's departure, Dana drives to a secluded spot, where she hugs her daughter, Flora, desperately, remarking that she is now the kind of mother she swore she would never be: one who, like her own, demands complete devotion and love. Chaurisse, unfortunately, is not much better off: she has, it seems, come to see Dana only to ensure that she really does now have her father all to herself. "Would you lie to me?" Chaurisse asks, after Dana confirms that she never sees James; when Dana insists that she is indeed telling the truth, Chaurisse leaves, satisfied that her hard-won nuclear family is once again sound (340). Neither woman has really come to terms with the devastation of their father's double life in ways that make room for sisterhood, and neither is anyone's heroine in the aftermath. As Dana remarks in the final lines: "What doesn't kill you doesn't kill you. That's all you get" (340). It seems that both women, in their own ways, have merely learned how to survive the trauma of their youth. They can offer no glittering pearls of wisdom or shining examples of forgiveness or magnanimity. They simply do the best they can.

Jones's second and fourth novels portray equally problematic familial bonds but specifically explore love relationships that buckle under the weight of circumstance and tragedy. In her second novel, *The Untelling* (2005), Aria Jackson is the product of a home broken by her father's death and her mother's erratic behavior, which grew increasingly volatile after losing her husband and baby daughter in a car accident. Aria comes of age harboring extreme guilt. On the day of the crash, she, a precocious ten-year-old, is forced to stay in the car while her mother and sister desperately try to save the youngest daughter, Genevieve. As a result, she watches her father die. When she cannot bear the sounds of his final cries, Aria covers her ears and sings nursery rhymes. "To the only man who ever loved me," she recalls, "I said 'I'm not listening. I can't hear you'" (9).

By the time she reaches adulthood, Aria has had her share of men and sorrow. She now lives in a dilapidated house with her best friend from college, Rochelle, who is everything Aria is not: beautiful, confident, and soon to be married to her true love, a successful dentist named Rod. Aria is now dating Dwayne, a locksmith whose desirability has much more to do with his pain than with Aria's physical or intellectual attraction to him. In fact, Dwayne is most appealing to her because he is "a father without his child," a young boy who lives in a different state, and she is "a child without her father." Somehow, thinks Aria, their meeting is fateful, and their union is ordained by these parallel fates alone (119).

Unfortunately, however, in her own haste to create a family separate from her mother, whose cruelty ultimately drives Aria's sister, Hermione, into an early marriage with their late father's best friend, Aria jumps at the possibility of being pregnant and only learns that she is, in fact, experiencing symptoms of early-onset menopause after she has mistakenly told Dwayne she is expecting. In response, Dwayne, unbeknownst to her, signs away his parental rights to his first child at the mother's request and agrees to marry Aria as soon as possible. As her name suggests, Aria's eagerness, which is traced back to her early loss, sets into motion a tragedy of Greek proportions. When she discovers her impending infertility, she cannot bear to reveal her mistake and instead tells Dwayne that she has miscarried, but he is eager to reconceive. When he discovers the truth, he leaves, and soon so too does Rochelle, who, frustrated by the stress of planning an elaborate wedding, elopes with her fiancé several months early. Aria is left in the crumbling house she loves with Rochelle's cat and her discarded wedding dress—two things Aria desperately wanted to keep, but now, without the husband with whom she wanted to re-create a "normal" family, she has no one with whom to share them.

Similarly, in *An American Marriage* (2018), Celestial Hamilton is shattered by an almost perfect life gone horribly wrong: her husband, a successful would-be entrepreneur, Roy, is wrongfully convicted of rape and sentenced to more than a decade in Louisiana's brutal prison system. Roy's conviction has devastating, rippling effects: Roy's mother, Olive, soon dies of both cancer and heartbreak, and Celestial unexpectedly becomes the breadwinner for her halved household, opening a boutique where she sells handmade dolls—a dream that was once a distant goal but is hastily realized after Roy's incarceration. Before his conviction, Celestial is a sassy but permissive wife; she forgives Roy's occasional affairs, and she supports his dream of "sitting his wife down," that is, becoming the household breadwinner and financing the couple's upper-middle-class lifestyle (43). However, when she is left to fend for herself in bustling Atlanta, she becomes resourceful, if not mercenary, in her fight for her and Roy's survival. Celestial's first indiscretion is her decision to make and sell dolls that allude to her husband's fate: the dolls are dressed in prison garb and bear a striking resemblance to Roy; however, as her fame in the art world increases, she never divulges to anyone that she is the wife of an inmate. Roy, in turn, feels both furious and slighted by his wife's silence. Several years later, she opens her boutique, Poupées, alone, though the venture was Roy's brainchild and plan before his arrest. Finally, after the horror of having to attend Olive's funeral without Roy, Celestial leans a bit too heavily on Andre, the couple's mutual friend, and their relationship blossoms into a full-on affair. By the time Roy is released from prison, the marriage is damaged beyond repair, and they ultimately part ways, with Celestial and Andre expecting their first child (a double blow, since Celestial terminated a pregnancy with Roy shortly after his conviction), and with Roy returning to Louisiana and Davina, a woman with whom he had a brief affair shortly after his release.

The Untelling and *An American Marriage* are both texts wherein Jones shines best in her portrayals of Black women characters who make life-altering mistakes, but who also, as Chris Rock states, come back and learn from them. By the end of *The Untelling*, Aria is learning to forgive herself, but she has also offered that gift to her mother, who, unbeknownst to anyone, blamed herself for Genevieve's death so many years before (the baby was sitting in her lap, and not in a car seat, during the crash). Celestial, who has tried to atone for her indiscretions by offering herself to Roy in their old bedroom, learns that she cannot make up for lost time by pretending that the past never happened. Roy forgives her, but he also offers her his prayers for her peace, which he tells her she must make for herself (306). In each case, the women cannot rebuild the past, but they can move forward into futures that acknowledge what has happened, as well as what is now possible in the aftermath of healing.

I tend to push back against the urge to make women—and particularly Black women—representative of concepts or ideas; such thinking sits at the root of the problematic characterizations Hill Collins identifies in the tropes mentioned earlier, but I wonder what we might gain from looking at the personal evolutions of characters like Aria and Celestial in the larger scheme of discussions about southern literature. As Jones herself points out in an interview with *Poets & Writers*, "Black writers are not really considered to be Southern writers. . . . 'Southern writing' is shorthand for an Old South that people are nostalgic about, but black people don't share that same nostalgia" (Spencer, "She Is Ready," 49). However, Tayari Jones's work makes a case for new paradigms, new conversations, and new representations that, like the women who emerge from *The Untelling* and *An American Marriage*, are no longer fettered by their own mistakes or afraid to acknowledge them in some vain attempt to retain respectability or ward off shame. Jones's decision to create them as such has implications that reach beyond the page and the narratives these women offer: they usher us into a new kind of telling of Black women's stories, but also of southern stories, ones wherein Black women are allowed to be as imperfect as they want to be, and free of the fear that those implications might tarnish an entire race. Critics would do well to take up more of Jones's work, further examining the ways that she speaks back to regional literature that has not always been kind to women like hers. We as critics are forever talking in circles about a "New South," with its new subjects and aesthetics. Well, Tayari Jones has been offering us one for nearly two decades. It's high time we picked up our pens.

Note

1. For more on these "controlling images," see Patricia Hill Collins, *Black Feminist Thought: Knowledge, Consciousness, and the Politics of Empowerment* (1990; New York: Routledge, 1991), particularly chap. 4, "Mammies, Matriarchs, and Other Controlling Images," 67–90.

Works Cited

Collins, Patricia Hill. *Black Feminist Thought: Knowledge, Consciousness, and the Politics of Empowerment*. 1990. New York: Routledge, 1991.

Fisher, Mike. "Daughters Get Their Day in Tayari Jones's *Silver Sparrow.*" *Pittsburgh Tribune*, June 2, 2011, 12.

Jacobs, Harriet. *Incidents in the Life of a Slave Girl, Written by Herself.* Boston: Thayer & Eldridge, 1861.

Jones, Tayari. *An American Marriage.* Algonquin, 2018.

Jones, Tayari. *Leaving Atlanta.* Warner, 2002.

Jones, Tayari. *The Untelling.* Grand Central, 2005.

Jones, Tayari. *Silver Sparrow.* Algonquin, 2011.

Morrison, Toni. *Sula.* Knopf, 1973.

Rock, Chris. "Chris Rock Explains the Only Way Black People Can Win in America." YouTube, uploaded by Thomas Sodomizer, November 13, 2014. https://www.youtube.com/watch?v=hCpL9m307eY. Accessed November 17, 2018.

Spencer, Rochelle. "She Is Ready: A Profile of Tayari Jones." *Poets & Writers*, May–June 2011, 45–49.

Washburn, Lindy. "Doomed Classes of Atlanta." *Bergen County Record*, January 4, 2004, E01.

Stephanie Powell Watts was born in Lenoir, North Carolina. After she earned her BA from the University of North Carolina at Charlotte and PhD from the University of Missouri, her family settled in Bethlehem, Pennsylvania, where she and her husband serve as faculty in Lehigh University's creative writing program. Since 2011, Watts has published one short story collection, *We Are Taking Only What We Need* (2011), and one novel, *No One Is Coming to Save Us* (2017). Her fiction, known for its unflinching and powerful explorations of African American experience in the American South, has won multiple awards, including a Pushcart Prize, a Whiting Award, the Ernest J. Gaines Award for Literary Excellence, and the Southern Women's Writers Award for Emerging Writer of the Year ("About Stephanie").

Home and the Myth of Reinvention in the Fiction of Stephanie Powell Watts

Melody Pritchard

Stephanie Powell Watts writes at a time when much fiction from the American South qualifies as "rough" or as "grit lit." Watts's work, on the other hand, while exploring deprivation and human suffering, is largely devoid of the violence and depravity that characterize typical Rough South fiction. Nevertheless, despite its less visceral depiction of violence, Watts's South remains decidedly hardscrabble. Her working-class characters struggle, often fruitlessly, in a world fraught with pain, longing, and isolating lack. Watts's work grapples with themes sitting at the heart of Rough South literature, but it does so in an original voice, one that departs from the gratuitousness and sensationalism of lesser writers.

Watts's first publication, a short story collection titled *We Are Taking Only What We Need* (2011), features working-class African American women living in North Carolina. Each of the ten stories focuses on different (usually poor) characters with decidedly different lives. The scope of representation in the collection points to Watts's prowess as a writer of Black cultural experience: her narrators range from Jehovah's Witness initiates and angry mothers to displaced daughters and empowered preteens. Regardless of their varied existences, each narrator's story circles closely around thematic territory common to southern fiction: home. For Watts's characters, "home" is much more than a mere dwelling. Home becomes a conceptual space that represents both the past and the possible future, an idealized image that shows a woman who she has been and who she could be. Home, then, evokes a familiar tension between the need for "roots" and the desire to escape those roots and become someone new, someone unburdened by the past. Thus the search for home doubles as the search for another destination well-known within both the American and southern imaginary: the horizon of individual reinvention. However, like many of her contemporaries, Watts refuses to produce fiction that simply reiterates threadbare cultural ideologies. Her collection recasts these common literary themes by creating characters capable of establishing individual destinies within the confines of loved but limiting collective histories.

The stories that Watts structures as a retelling or recollection of a narrator's childhood experiences are especially emblematic of the ways in which Watts refashions the familiar tension between belonging and individual freedom. The collection's opening story, "Family Museum of the Ancient Postcards," chronicles the late-in-life love affair of Aunt Ginny and Gerald as narrated by Ginny's unnamed relative, fourteen years old at the time. The opening paragraphs make it apparent that Aunt Ginny's newfound love comes as a shock to the family, who "[gave] up on her long, long ago" and assume she will forever live a life of spinsterhood (2). Along with shock, Aunt Ginny's family members also look on her relationship as ultimately futile, firm in their belief that "late marriages can't take," and "Aunt Ginny's story [will] take one of just a few predictable shapes" (5). By carrying on with Gerald in search of a new life and home, Aunt Ginny balks at her family's expectations for her life. The story's narrator describes Aunt Ginny's determination as a "stretching for something good . . . [for] that glad day when the life with Gerald that she knew was just around the corner finally materialized, poof, in a cloud of sorcerer's smoke" (5). Although Aunt Ginny's quest for love is ultimately a failure, her desire to write her own life seemingly lives on with her niece, who, at the end of the story, manages to do what the other women in her family could not and rids the family home of their patriarch's ghostly presence.

In the collection's title piece, the narrator, Portia, recalls an event from the summer of her eleventh year that shaped her understanding of her father and herself. The story focuses on the summer after Portia's mother "moved out of Daddy's house to an apartment across town" (50). Her father, Roger, quickly takes up with the children's white teenage babysitter, Tammy, and their union results in disaster: in an attempt at revenge against Tammy for cheating on him, Roger shoots Tammy's favorite puppy and leaves it bloody on the doorstep of her and her family's home. Portia remarks that, at the time, she hated her father for this act, but she later comes to a different way to understand it:

> If I learned nothing else, I learned that love demands tribute. And whatever else you can say about crazy love, it is tenacious, it must be hyperbolic to survive or cooler heads, wise people with good sense—practical sorts who never find themselves drunk, crying, and stupid in the middle of the road— all those people and their boring practical reasonableness . . . they win. And if that happens, love never gets the chance to look you in the eyes, inches from your face, never gets to say, *Let me, let me, let me. You won't regret it. Let me.* Oh, Daddy, forgive me. I have been a fool. (71)

Here Portia revises her painful memories of her father by repurposing them into something useful, something that helps her make sense of moments in her life that are otherwise nonsensical. Once again, a character possesses inventive agency over her past and present selves without subjugating one to the other. Just as the narrator in "Family Museum of the Ancient Postcards" uses her memory of Aunt Ginny's story to understand where she comes from and what she is capable of, so Portia uses her recollection of a traumatic moment to connect with and understand her father and herself. Both protagonists navigate their pasts in creative ways that allow their histories to shape—but not define—who they are and how they live their lives. This subtle shift creates the possibility of belonging to a collective familial history without becoming a mere repository for it.

"Welcome to the City of Dreams" also speaks to themes of self and belonging, but it focuses specifically on reinvention as the desire to escape the consequences of history and start anew. In this piece, a mother, Nora, leaves her husband, packs up her young children, and heads out for a "whole new life" in the big city (111). On the drive to their new home, Nora assures her reluctant daughter that she will "like it here. . . . A big place like this, you can have anything you ever wanted" (108). While life in the city allows Nora to "get out of the life that was holding her back" (109) and start over in a place where "[everything] is new" (126), her daughter, Tash, finds herself in an "unhappy, unknowable" world (127). Ultimately Tash and her brother choose to return to their father's house in the country. When pulling away from Nora's apartment, an adult Tash recalls how "coming back to that place was the furthest thing from my mind. I wouldn't turn around. There is no way I could stand to see my mother's body rushing backward, receding from me until she vanished from my mind" (136). Tash realizes her decision to return home irrevocably fractures her connection to her mother. Tash sees Nora "a few times" in the following years, but she and her brother eventually "[lose] track of her" (136). Nora is cut from her family and lost to the empty promise of the big city. Nora's fate exposes the sharper edges that the romance of unbounded reinvention tends to hide, thereby undercutting more conventional iterations of the myth. Up to this point, a troubled version of the reinvention myth maps readily across the piece. Had the story ended here, it would have become an exploration of a timeworn but pervasive ideological construct's impact on contemporary American experience. However, the story continues until Tash accepts her mother's actions and effectively disrupts the easy unfolding of the reinvention myth:

> I do know that she thinks of us. Though I doubt she could afford to spend every single day doing it. No matter what, you have to figure out how to live in the day you have, not the ones you can't get back. Soon, I may look her up, just to let her know how things turned out. That she doesn't have to feel bad about anything. That life runs in different speeds depending on the situation and some times and days and moments get away from you before you really know what's what. . . . I'd tell her I wouldn't mind being her friend. . . . I wouldn't talk about missing her or sad old times, or the hours we spent explaining her to ourselves and especially not the quiet nights in the dark trying the best we knew how to remember anything she ever did or said that made us laugh. (137–38)

Tash's unprompted forgiveness of, and proposed reconciliation with, her mother create a stumbling block for analysis that relies on the reinvention myth to shoulder the heaviest interpretive work. When allowed to wander outside a critical paradigm that favors reinvention, focus shifts away from large, overarching commentary on cultural myths and loosens the reinvention myth's grip on both Nora's character and the story itself.

Watts continues to explore conceptions of home and reinvention with her debut novel, *No One Is Coming to Save Us* (2017). Characterized as a "loose retelling" of *The Great Gatsby* (Farmer, "A Force of Nature"), the novel chronicles a young man's homecoming and the life-altering effects it sets into motion. Set in a declining factory town in North Carolina, the plot is steeped in the myth of reinvention. After a long, mysterious absence, JJ Ferguson returns home with a familiar agenda: build a house; win back his lost love, Ava; and re-create his chance at the life he envisions. When Ava's mother, Sylvia, tells JJ of her now-married daughter's life, he remains stubbornly optimistic about the possibility of revising the past:

> "Life goes on. I know it has to. But that other life that we already went through, it might come back. . . ."
>   "All I'm saying is we only know about the past. Why not redo it?" (94)

Sylvia laughs and says, "You went away from here and lost your mind" (94), but she does not simply dismiss his claims as idle talk. She recognizes that JJ's return is fueled by a naive reliance on "the power of reinvention (in the redo, the most childish of all rules in any game)" (94–95) and cautions against this "ridiculous long shot," saying, "I don't want you to count on it. Make sure you aren't counting on it" (101).

The determination with which JJ pursues his ill-fated plan indicates a desperate desire to reduce the devastating lack pervading the lives and minds of the novel's characters. While JJ's quest may be the most drastic, Sylvia and Ava also go to great lengths to fill the "hollow spaces" (23) left by the "sting of not having or not having enough" (3). Sylvia carries on a long-term telephone friendship with a random young prisoner named Marcus, who reminds her of her long-dead son, and Ava obsesses over the idea of having a baby, but nothing alleviates the painful isolation created by years of lack and loneliness. Ava, in particular, notes the irrevocable gap between beings. When reflecting on her deteriorating marriage to Henry, she thinks, "[Every] once in a while you get reminded how truly impossible it is to know another person, even if you love that person, even if you live with him for years, for decades" (112). The shock of Henry's infidelity intensifies Ava's awareness of humans' inherent strangeness, and this sensitivity spills into her other relationships. In a moment of insight, Ava looks at her Aunt Lana and wonders "how she could have known her aunt all of her life and not known a damn thing about her" (164). Later she reflects on one of the most developed and fundamental relationships in the novel: the connection with her mother. Ava thinks, "[The] inside and secret places of another person's life are never palatable, especially your mother's life" (217). This insight becomes particularly poignant in light of how closely it mirrors Sylvia's earlier admission about "[feeling] unknown in the world, like she sleepwalked unconnected and alone" (98). Further, near the end of the novel, Ava dreams of her mother: "She is dreaming she knows for sure because she sees her mother, not just glances at her in periphery but she feels her mother's struggle to reach them. . . . How had Ava ever missed that struggle?" (338). Though Ava's dream allows her to see her mother's memory more directly, the text makes it clear that she "cannot talk to her mother, cannot signal to her or touch her" (338); even within her dream, Ava remains unreachable and separate from those closest to her.

Along with the lack created by humans' utter isolation, economic lack also drives these characters. Sylvia and Ava, while more economically sound than many working-class characters represented within the genre, still contend with money problems and the struggles of class. Sylvia and her husband, Don, raise Ava in a "small brick split-level" (23) house on Development Drive that, though nothing like the mansion JJ builds on nearby Brushy Mountain Road, is a "remarkable [step] up from ramshackle old clapboard houses, sagging porches, or old rusted trailers" in which she spent her childhood (19). Ava follows a similar upward-moving class trajectory and surpasses the status of her parents, landing a job as a "senior loan officer . . . with a real office all to herself" (26) and thereby earning her place as "a member (a new member for sure) . . . of the middle class" (27). Their family's economic progression illustrates the particularly poignant paradox of class mobility for the working class: while they can progress and move closer to the mansion on the hill, they can rarely occupy it.

For a brief moment, JJ's redo seems to bridge this gap and achieve the impossible: he builds his mansion on Brushy Mountain Road and gets his dream girl out of her husband's bed and into his. Standing in his new living room, "Jay smiled at Sylvia, then at Ava. He had waited for this very moment and it had happened. . . . Not many people get a taste of that feeling—getting just what you want just when you want it" (230–31). His success, though, does not hold. Ava realizes her love for JJ, though real and important to her, is not the kind one calls on to build homes and raise children. Ultimately, JJ's quest to remake himself, to "be the hero in his own story" and escape the consequences of the past, fails (89). Ava and Sylvia—though each remains rooted to her personal histories and failures—fare better. At the novel's conclusion, Ava fulfills her goal of becoming a mother by adopting children; Sylvia visits Marcus in prison and symbolically begins moving on from her son's death; and JJ's love for Ava haunts him until he dies while dreaming of her—only in death is the past "finally behind him" (367). The endings to these characters' stories illustrate Watts's ability to take an American literary theme, place it in a southern setting, and make it do something different: instead of reiterating the traditional American desire to reinvent oneself outside the confines of the past, Watts shows how that desire is empty and can never be satisfied.

While the novel's title makes it clear that no one is waiting to deliver deus ex machina moments, its characters' experiences suggest that a different type of redemption rests in the people one chooses to love. Near the end of the novel, Sylvia reflects on the inherent suffering that living brings, and how "[there] is an instinct to hide, and against our better thinking we find the darkest place to squeeze ourselves into. Someone has to be able to find you on those days. Somebody has to pull you out" (294). For these characters, there is always someone waiting to "pull you out" and remind you to "[fight] for your life" and continue on (293). Though Watts's characters are doubtless flawed, the most fulfilled ones love fiercely and unconditionally, and they are tireless in their attempts to care for and forgive one another. In this novel, salvation lives not in escape and reinvention but in our deepest moments, when—like Marcus when Sylvia finally and unexpectedly visits him in prison—we can look up from the darkness and say, "I can't believe you're here" (364).

Works Cited

"About Stephanie." Stephanie Powell Watts. https://stephaniepowellwatts.com/about. Accessed January 10, 2019.

Farmer, Casey. "'A Force of Nature': Stephanie Powell Watts Finds Success with First Novel." *Brown and White*, October 1, 2017. https://thebrownandwhite.com/2017/10/01/lehigh -stephanie-powell-watts-profile. Accessed January 10, 2019.

Watts, Stephanie Powell. *No One Is Coming to Save Us*. HarperCollins, 2017.

Watts, Stephanie Powell. *We Are Taking Only What We Need*. HarperCollins, 2011.

Brian Panowich is an award-winning author, a Georgia fire-fighter, and a father of four. His first novel, *Bull Mountain*, topped the best thriller list of 2015 on Apple iBooks, placed in the top twenty best books of 2015 on Amazon, and went on to win the International Thriller Writers Award for Best First Novel (2016), as well as the Pat Conroy Award (formerly the SIBA Award) for Best Mystery (2016). The book was also nominated for the Barry Award, the Anthony Award, and the Georgia Townsend Book Prize and was a finalist for the 2016 LA Times Book Prize. His second novel, *Like Lions*, was released in 2018. His third, *Hard Cash Valley*, appeared in 2020.

Brian Panowich
Music of the Country

Jay Varner

In the paperback release of his debut novel, *Bull Mountain*, Brian Panowich writes that he is of the "firm opinion that there is not much noticeable difference" between songs and novels. "They both need to flow," he believes, "and to pace themselves in order to get across to their audience with the proper tension, and they both share a rhythmic quality, a melody even" (294). Set in the dark, secluded woods of North Georgia, *Bull Mountain* largely explores several generations of the Burroughs family's always evolving and always illicit criminal enterprise. The violent, sprawling narrative does not flow as much as it tumbles like a rockslide after a shocking opening chapter. Tension builds among an interconnected cast of brutal moonshiners, frantic meth addicts, and haunted law enforcement officers. All of it is done with a deft literary prowess; if we were to follow the formula that music and novels share, it is clear that Panowich practices what he preaches on the page.

Panowich, who spent over a decade touring as a musician, curated an exhaustive Spotify playlist that he dubbed a *Bull Mountain* soundtrack. Son Volt, American Aquarium, Sturgill Simpson, the White Buffalo, and Sons of Bill are just a few of the soundtrack artists who fall under the expansive, undefinable umbrella of a genre known as outlaw country. In what other type of country would any of Panowich's hillbilly noir stories take place? The more a reader knows about this music, the richer Panowich's novel becomes. The small town where much of *Bull Mountain* takes place? Waymore Valley, an Easter egg for any reader who knows the 1975 Waylon Jennings classic "Waymore's Blues." However, this is one of the more overt references. In fact, the most consistent allusions involve more than just naming names. Panowich connects on a deeper spiritual level with the music. Outlaw country is perhaps most easily exemplified by Johnny Cash flipping the bird to the camera, by Willie Nelson wearing a red bandana and ponytail, by Waylon Jennings growing lonesome, ornery, and mean while bucking the Nashville record establishment and making the music he wants. Panowich seems to have done the same, writing the novel he sought to write, telling the fictional stories about characters and settings that capture the truth.

Back in the '70s, so the legend goes, the outlaws all sought to stay true to their musical roots within country yet embraced a hard-living lifestyle that was usually found in rock and roll. Oh, sure, alcohol, drugs, and sex were always present in country music, but that fact was hardly a selling point to the mainstream audiences Nashville had calculated they could attract. After the 1960s, record execs could not fathom a version of country music that featured long hair, debauchery, and politics. What would the silent majority think? Nashville needed carefully marketed artists who captured the kind of safe and wholesome message that the average listener in Oklahoma could get behind. Hell, Merle Haggard satirized—and cashed in—that very idea with "Okie from Muskogee."

The problem, as Dana Jennings writes in *Sing Me Back Home: Love, Death, and Country Music*, is that "with the deepest country music, there are no casual listeners" (10). Nashville's sanitized version bleached out the complexities that had always made country music so compelling. The audience might grow, but the music is no different from drinking diluted whiskey: a weak approximation of the original. And just what is the real thing? "The music is curse and redemption, the journey and the homeplace, current events and ancient tales," Jennings continues. "The music is prayer and litany, epiphany and salvation" (10).

In Martin Scorsese's masterful concert film *The Last Waltz* (1976), the drummer Levon Helm looks back to his musical roots, trying to define not only the Band but their unique style of music. Today, the Band is viewed as one of the cornerstones of the genre. Acts such as the Byrds, the Flying Burrito Brothers, and the Grateful Dead occupy the same landscape on our

Mount Rushmore of outlaw country. But when it first started, nobody—not even Helm—knew what to call it.

"Bluegrass or country music," Levon says, exhaling cigarette smoke. "If it mixes there with rhythm, and if it dances, then you've got a combination of all those different kinds of music. Country, bluegrass, blues music, show music." Off camera, Scorsese asks, "What's it called, then?" Without missing a beat, Levon smiles and says, "Rock and roll."

Outlaw country is a little bit of everything, in the same way that American music is a hodgepodge of cultures, histories, attitudes, and musicians. Then again, any debate around a definition of this subgenre fits perfectly within the overall inability to even define the mother genre of country music. At the start of his seminal book *Country Music U.S.A.*, the music scholar Bill C. Malone seeks to define this seam of music so deeply buried inside southern identity. "It is a vigorous hybrid form of music," Malone writes, "constantly changing and growing in complexity, just as the society in which it thrives also matures and evolves" (1).

The many narratives woven together inside *Bull Mountain* echo a similar evolution. In the novel's earliest narrative, set in 1949, the moonshining Burroughs family drives the same lonely stretches of the lost highway Hank Williams sang about (his version of the song was also released in 1949) and are similarly damned to pay the cost for a life of sin. By the novel's end in 2015, the remaining members of the Burroughs clan resemble any of the haunted and scarred characters in the Drive-By Truckers' brooding modern southern rock songs. The contemporary narrative strands, just like the progression from "true" country music, are louder and fuzzed out from the increasing distortion imposed by the modern world; but pull at the threads long enough, and you eventually get back to the same type of darkness that has always been woven into the fabric of country music. On a website post for the *Writer's Bone* literary podcast network, Panowich writes, "Like everything else in my life, *Bull Mountain*, the novel, wouldn't exist without the music that inspired me to write it. It flows through the whole story."

The Burroughs family falls well within the bounds of the outlaw. In the most literal sense, they are cold and hardened criminals. None of the laws the family members deem worthy of following appears in any constitution or rule book. Their law follows a pure and cruel version of justice and fairness that is true to what their ancestors delivered atop Bull Mountain. Their criminal enterprise delivers wealth and power to the family, yet it thrusts them into a world of ceaseless violence that is often kill or be killed. Even the criminality of the Burroughs clan mimics that push-pull relationship between tradition and the future.

For the first fifty years of the twentieth century, the Burroughses made a handsome living off moonshine. Panowich is smart enough to pay tribute to one of Appalachia's most common criminal tropes, the moonshiner. In fact, drink enough liquor, and it would be easy to imagine the Burroughses facing off against the moonshining forefathers Matt Bondurant writes about in his real-life novel *The Wettest County in the World*. But Panowich is also interested in progress and evolution. What arrives once Prohibition ends and interstate commerce slowly floods even rural Georgia? As liquor proves less and less profitable, the Burroughses are forced to make a choice.

Rye hopes to move toward legitimacy through "working smarter, not harder." He tries to convince his brother Cooper that the first step on this path is selling timber rights to the family acreage. Cooper has a different idea: marijuana. Ultimately, it's a bullet from Cooper's rifle that wins the argument. Over the next several decades, Cooper, his son Gareth, and his grandsons Halford and Buckley expand the business into the illegal gun trade and methamphetamine. Their enterprise expands from good ole local boys to dangerous Florida bikers. Time passes: guns become larger and deadlier, the drugs become more varied and potent, cell phones lasso characters to their work. Progress and evolution—yet the results of moral rot are always the same. And the Burroughses, just like Cooper, refuse to change. Adapt? Sure, they can add weed and crank to the alcohol. But that's just market demand. Hardly a change.

No song better captures the insular world and determined attitude of the Burroughses than "Never Gonna Change," Jason Isbell's most raucous contribution from his early years with the Drive-By Truckers. The song's drug-dealing narrator begins with a warning to an unnamed girl who has come to a place populated with men "mean and strong like liquor" that if she's here to work on reforming him, she best be on her way. The mantra-like chorus repeats again and again, "We ain't never gonna change / We ain't doin' nothin' wrong / We ain't never gonna change / So shut your mouth and play along." It's the same type of ultimatum—largely unspoken—that Gareth Burroughs gives to his sweetheart, Annette. She'd heard stories about the violent history atop Bull Mountain, and it is easy to see why she would be drawn to a confident yet dangerous man like Gareth. Serving as a kind of partner to Gareth seemed exciting. Besides, as a native of the area, she understands the lesson of shutting up and doing what needs to be done.

A dozen years and three sons later, Annette realizes that her expected role is no different from that of generations of Georgia mountain women: a housekeeper and mother and someone to satisfy her husband's drunken, violent sexual urges. It is clear from the hard lessons Gareth instills, along with the hardened gaze of their grandfather Cooper, that the only future her sons have will take place on that mountain.

Annette leaves without so much as even a note. She is never to be seen again by their three sons. And Gareth, to again steal a line from Isbell's song, has few regrets: "But there ain't much difference in the man I wanna be and the man I really am." The fate of a family's rot, the murderous destiny of locality, and the hardness of a never satisfied world have shaped Gareth into the type of calloused man that he always wanted and needed to become.

Mostly.

When a prostitute asks about the Annette tattoo on his chest, Gareth slices the woman's face with a broken liquor bottle. But her scars run deeper than the skin. Unbeknownst to her, she is pregnant with Gareth's son—and that boy will struggle for years as he grows up with a drug-addicted single mother who strips and turns tricks to survive. If each of us decides which song we're going to sing, Simon Holly decided early on that his would be about revenge. He rolls into Waymore Valley as an outsider and an FBI agent. He's just a stranger who has come to enforce the law. Nobody knows that he shares the fierce, sadistic blood of the Burroughses. Perhaps the only noble part of that blood is the loyalty and commitment the Burroughses hold for each other. Sure, Holly seeks to murder all his half brothers and bring down a multistate drug-running operation, but it's all to avenge his mother. Here, again, Panowich harkens back to one of the classic threads in country music: revenge. Simon Holly isn't named Sue, but it's easy to see that the lessons his father taught him might not necessarily be what he imagined.

How does one deal with the inheritance of violence inflicted on others? One of the constant themes and messages of the novel is that you either confront the past or spend a lifetime failing to push it down, damned to repeat the same melody until the end. It's a cycle of male toxicity and violence that we have seen again and again, from the rural South of Flannery O'Connor to the snowy Adirondacks in Russell Banks's *Affliction*. Especially potent in the patriarchal culture of Bull Mountain is the worship of men. In turn, men destroy each other and themselves.

For Cooper, the ghosts of the past—along with years of alcohol abuse—decay his brain. Rye's murder seems like a low-level hum that never fully leaves his consciousness. It is among the same woods where he murdered and then buried Rye that Cooper turns the gun on himself to submit to the darkness for good. Cooper's son Gareth finds his father's body and spends a lifetime trying to become the same type of cold-blooded thief and murderer. That ambition takes him to great heights until it all blows up in his face. When the family begins baking meth through trial and error, it's Gareth who pours the wrong ingredient and explodes along with the cook shed. Buckley's taste for, and withdrawal from, the family's crank ends up costing him his life, gunned down by federal agents—though not before confessing everything to an FBI agent by the name of Simon Holly. After Buckley's death, Halford assumes leadership of the family. Halford's death is all but certain from the novel's outset; the only question is who will pull the trigger and when. Will it be Agent Holly? Or perhaps the town sheriff, Clayton Burroughs?

Clayton is the only son of Gareth and Annette who has tried to escape the family's long and bloody history. Although he is a law officer, he has also chosen to look the other way over what his family does. As he explains it, "I'm a hick sheriff in a small town doing my best to keep the people of this valley—the *good* people of the valley—safe from the never-ending river of shit that flows down that mountain" (26).

Yet that same Burroughs blood flows through him, so it's an added irony that Clayton's preferred method of anesthetizing himself was the original shit that flowed down that mountain: alcohol. Whereas he was once a hard drinker, by the time we meet him, Clayton has cleaned up his ways, thanks in part to his wife, Kate. But this is a noir novel, and set in Georgia. Sobriety is always a hard and finite fight. As Clayton starts craving that burn in his throat, it's only a matter of time before "there stands the glass."

Panowich claims that the inspiration for Clayton stems from the opening line to the Band's "Up on Cripple Creek": "When I get off of this mountain, you know where I wanna go?" Clayton's long climb down that mountain meant not only distancing himself from the family land and business but joining the opposite side: law enforcement. It's bad enough that Clayton turned his back on the family business—and all the worse that he is bound

by law to stop that family. Halford's explosive contempt for his brother comes
as no surprise. However, it has long been a part of their relationship.

"But it ain't like we all didn't see it coming," Halford tells Clayton at one
point. "Ever since you were a kid, you walked around thinking you were better
than us, and now look at you, strutting around with that star on your shirt,
still trying to prove how much better than us you are" (143).

Clayton's struggle is similar to the one described in an old mountain
bluegrass song called "Don't Get above Your Raisin." The song alludes to the
American myth that each of us can ascend from our birthplace and live a
life—financially, educationally—better than that of our parents. However,
here's the rub: living out that myth is perceived as insolence. The song suggests
that roots, community, family, and commonality are all more important than
a drive for success. When we climb up in social class, that trajectory creates
an overwhelming fear for those who can't or—more commonly—choose not
to follow. They believe we have forsaken our families in the process. If we do
pull the tent posts and strike out for greener pastures, we will not only forget
where we came from but also grow ashamed of our upbringing.

And ultimately, none of the characters in this story can fully escape the
past of their fathers—or mothers. The violence and evils of our parents sift
down through generations in ways we can never comprehend. The Burroughs
men are deeply damaged by the compounding sins of their bloodlines. As
Clayton describes it, Halford has become nearly unrecognizable, a kingpin
operating solely by rote memory. Early in the novel, when FBI agent Holly
first arrives in Waymore Valley to discuss using money as a way of turning
Halford, Clayton pushes back: "You don't understand how it works up here,"
he explains to the agent. "Money isn't the endgame for my brother. It never
was. It's simply a by-product of the lifestyle my father raised him on" (29).

Agent Holly still doesn't quite grasp the hold this way of life has on the
Burroughses—or if he does, he doesn't let Clayton in on the secret. Holly has
flipped and caught many criminals; Halford Burroughs can't be that different.
"Up here it's something different," Clayton insists. "It's something deeper than
bone. It's not something that they earned or had to fight to get. They were
born into it, and the fight comes on real hard when someone threatens to
take it away. It's an integral part of who they are—who we are" (31).

Family is the first word of the novel—and those themes obviously run
throughout. We see the threads of family play out in the history of country
music: Hank Williams Sr., Jr., and III; Waylon and Shooter Jennings; Steve

Earle and his son Justin Townes Earle; and of course the Carter and Cash families. In the most literal of senses, we see the shared blood of family—but family is more than relatives. It's community, fellowship, shared experiences. Choctaw, one of Clayton's deputies—his only deputy, in fact—is a veteran of Iraq and, late in the novel, is roped into a doomed scheme to rob dealers and gun runners connected to the Burroughses. When Clayton confronts him, Choctaw says he only agreed with the plan because his former military buddy asked, that he was desperate for cash and bound out of obligation. They're family.

Clayton is working to build his own family, even though it was his stupid, blind love for Kate that is now risking so much. One day at the local diner, after word spread that the current sheriff was stepping down, Kate said, "You should run, Clayton. You'd make a great sheriff" (47). It seems neither of them fully realized what it meant to be a husband who is a cop and to be a cop's wife and be kept up at night with worry when he's not home safe. But even though Clayton wears the badge, Kate wears enough confidence for everyone in McFalls County. When a stranger brings Clayton home in a different car, Kate shows up at the door, holding a shotgun.

The progression of female characters is integral to the story. While Annette is stoic throughout her relationship with Gareth, she ultimately slips away without firing a shot. Kate, on the other hand, would never pass quietly into the night. She is like a badass Loretta Lynn character who left "Fist City" for even bigger fights. And you'd better believe that, by novel's end, the biggest win of all belongs to Kate. The ending offers a scant glimmer of hope: perhaps the circle of male violence has finally been broken. Then again, Kate's final act—gunning down Agent Holly—is the same type of violence that has plagued the Burroughses for a century. The more things change . . .

The website Saving Country Music features a banner epigraph that reads: "When a culture's music is lifeless, that culture is bound for more trouble than just having nothing decent to listen to." And it's hard to argue against that. The grit, the heart, and the realness—they're gone from the mainstream. We try to find it in other corners. Panowich writes on *Writer's Bone* that in his youth, he shrugged off his father's beloved outlaw country in favor of Van Halen, the Ramones, and Bruce Springsteen. He spent years "armed with three chords and the truth." But in the end, like the Burroughses' connection to their mountain, he returned. "It was a natural progression for me," he says. "Like father like son, from the punch-in-the-face of rock-and-roll to the snide swagger of Americana and country." Outlaw country, rock and roll, Americana—whatever you call this music, it's alive inside *Bull Mountain*.

Works Cited

The Band. "Up on Cripple Creek." *The Band*. Capital, 1969.

Bondurant, Matt. *The Wettest County in the World: A Novel Based on a True Story*. Scribner, 2008.

Coroneos, Kyle. Saving Country Music. 2008. https://www.savingcountrymusic.com. Accessed November 12, 2018.

Drive-By Truckers. "Never Gonna Change." *The Dirty South*. New West Records, 2008.

Flatt and Scruggs. "Don't Get above Your Raisin." Columbia, 1951.

Jennings, Dana. *Sing Me Back Home: Love, Death, and Country Music*. Faber & Faber, 2008.

The Last Waltz. Directed by Martin Scorsese. With performances by the Band, Bob Dylan, Neil Young, Van Morrison, and Eric Clapton. United Artists, 1978.

Lynn, Loretta. "Fist City." *Fist City*. Decca Records, 1968.

Malone, Bill C., and Jocelyn R. Neal. *Country Music, U.S.A.* 3rd ed. University of Texas Press, 2010.

Panowich, Brian. "Author Brian Panowich on How Musical Exploration Fueled His Writing." *Writer's Bone*, May 13, 2015. https://www.writersbone.com/writing-playlist/2015/5/13/author-brian-panowich-on-how-musical-exploration-fueled-his-writing. Accessed August 1, 2018.

Panowich, Brian. *Bull Mountain*. Putnam, 2015.

Panowich, Brian. *Like Lions*. Head of Zeus, 2018.

Williams, Hank. "Lost Highway." MGM, 1949.

Ravi Howard, a native of Montgomery, Alabama, is assistant professor of creative writing and African American narratives at Florida State University. He holds a BA in journalism from Howard University and an MFA from the University of Virginia, where he was editor in chief of the literary publication *Meridian*. As a journalist, he has written and produced programs on several sports networks, winning an Emmy in 2004 for his contribution to HBO's *Inside the NFL*. His short stories have appeared in *Salon* and *Massachusetts Review*. The essay ". . . And Mourning Jubilee" was published in 2010 in the *New York Times*; the essay "Elevator Music" appears in the anthology *Children of the Changing South*. To date he has published two novels: *Like Trees, Walking* (2007) and *Driving the King* (2015). His first novel won the Ernest J. Gaines Award for Literary Excellence and was a finalist for the Hemingway Foundation / PEN Award and the Hurston-Wright Legacy Award for Debut Fiction. Howard has received fellowships and awards from the National Endowment for the Arts, Hurston-Wright Foundation, Bread Loaf Writers' Conference, and the New Jersey State Council of the Arts.

"The Heart of the Matter"
Blending Fiction and History

Bes Stark Spangler

Born in 1975 and growing up in Montgomery, Alabama, Ravi Howard heard stories of civil rights demonstrations, the Montgomery bus boycott, Martin Luther King's efforts, and even, through reports from extended family members, the 1981 lynching of Michael Donald in Mobile, Alabama. Howard's interest in history, particularly southern African American history, results, in part, from hearing these stories. "History was just always present . . . [and] remembering these stories told by 'ordinary people' . . . had an impact on my story telling," he acknowledges. In a short essay, "Elevator Music," he emphasizes the importance of preserving artifacts and historical sites as well as stories and documents as he shares his meaningful memory of having his hair cut, sitting in the barber's chair where Martin Luther King Jr. once sat (161).

Comfortable with his identity as a writer of urban historical fiction, Howard responded "yes" to Tayari Jones's question, asked during a recorded conversation, about whether he considers himself a southern writer; however, he immediately provided a more nuanced answer: "I prefer the idea of layers of labeling. We can define ourselves with those layers. Black writer. Southern writer. Some folks are Urban Southern. Historical Southern. Gulf Coastal writers. Layers give you specificity. And you can use as many layers as you need to get to the heart of the matter" (Howard, "In Conversation").

When Michel Martin asked, during an NPR interview after the publication of *Like Trees, Walking*, if Howard has considered the reaction of white readers to his work, he responded, "These are moments in history that happened. And we can't necessarily be ashamed of things that happened in our past, because I don't think there's any shame in discussing history or reflecting a fully textured version of American history" (Howard, "Novelist Ravi Howard"). That his two novels center on racially motivated acts of violence indicates that he intends his focus on African American history not only to reveal the responses of "ordinary" people to violent events but also to show that the "fully textured version" of southern history includes enmity and injustice.

Howard's interest in researching "full textures" led him first to Howard University and later to the MFA program at the University of Virginia, where he was editor in chief of the literary magazine *Meridian*. For his master's thesis, he submitted the short story "Like Trees, Walking." In his conversation with Tayari Jones, he recalls that writing about Mobile brought his youthful memories of Alabama into sharper focus (Howard, "In Conversation"). To verify facts as well as memories, however, he visited Mobile, familiarizing himself with the locations he would include in the novel, including its Jubilee tradition, which he described in a piece for the *New York Times*:

> On a few nights each summer—no one knows precisely when—the waters of Mobile Bay push thousands of fish and crabs onto the shores around Daphne. Decaying leaves and sediment from the Mobile-Tensaw River Delta flow into the bay, lowering the water's oxygen level. The fish stop swimming and float to the surface. Most of them end up on the beach, stunned but alive and ready to be harvested.
>
> Word spreads quickly, and people from Daphne and the surrounding cities crowd onto the shore to collect the free seafood. It is a rare, unpredictable moment that happens nowhere else but Mobile Bay. ("... And Mourning Jubilee")

The epigraph of the novel *Like Trees, Walking* (2007) refers readers to the title's biblical source, Mark 8:24, which tells of a blind man's initial response to Jesus's healing touch. In a blurred vision, the man sees "men, like trees, walking." A second touch fully restores his sight. Though taken from the New Testament, the title does not indicate a religious allegory. Rather than advancing a "message" (although the novel emphasizes the immorality of racial hatred), the story's impact results largely from the irony of setting, both of time and of place. Implied associations suggest "layers" of possibilities: a body hanging from the branch of a tree—the city of Mobile is known for its trees—and thematic associations with sight and insight.

The novel might have been a coming-of-age story of two brothers, Roy and Paul Deacon, living seemingly secure lives in a respectable middle-class Mobile community. Instead it becomes a record of their awakening to the reality of racial hatred lingering under the civilized surface of Mobile society. Howard focuses on the effects of this awakening through the memory of Roy Deacon, who, in 1981, was a seventeen-year-old high school senior. In the prologue, Roy appears as a reflective man soon to turn forty, the seventh-generation owner and director of Deacon Funeral Home. As he remembers the summers he and Paul waited on the beach for the Mobile Bay Jubilee, he recalls in particular the spring of 1981, thus beginning the memoir, presented in the form of two books. Assuming the voice of his younger self, he presents in book 1 the weeklong events after the lynching of Michael Donald, each chapter covering one day. Book 2 is shorter; chapters are designated by holidays, indicating the passage of time as people continue to seek justice while living normal lives.

A skeptical youth who willingly conforms to family expectations but keeps his own counsel, Roy questions the existence of God. He attends church but confesses that he gets more from the music than from the sermons. He is wise beyond his years, yet he shares in the activities and interests of his friends and goes steady with Lorraine, the girl he will eventually marry. Howard's skill in depicting scenes, actions, and moods through Roy's observations and memories provides a palpable sense of reality. In the pages devoted to the Monday after the Saturday crime, Howard depicts the events through Roy's observations and responses. Arriving at school, Roy stops to speak with Mr. Barrett, the groundskeeper who is changing the events sign to memorialize Michael Donald, class of 1980. Barrett says, "That Donald boy was good people. Never caused no trouble or nothing. . . . Stringing folks up. Thought all of that was water under the bridge. I guess it ain't" (69).

In homeroom, Roy sits quietly with the other seniors as Mrs. Randolph sits "with her hands clasped too tight to be comfortable," taking roll silently by looking directly at each student (70). Moving from class to class, Roy observes that "the lynching had settled into everything like smoke" (71), but later in the day, when he and friends gather in the parking lot, the tempo and language quicken. Discussing afternoon activities that will allow them to be home early, the youths attempt to cover their fear with bravado: "My daddy gave me his pistol," Slim says. "He keeps it under the seat."

"But Michael was walking," I said. "Gun won't do you any good under the seat."
"That's why I got it on me." Slim reached over and clutched his book bag. (72)

When Lorraine arrives, Buster greets her by saying, "Hey Lorraine. . . . I asked your girl Naomi to the prom and she looked at me like I was crazy" (74). The banter continues until Roy and Lorraine get into his car. When Lorraine asks Roy to drive to the scene of the hanging, he reluctantly does so and watches as she takes her rosary in hand and gets out of the car to pray. Finally arriving at her house, they see Lorraine's mother, sitting on the porch, anxiously overseeing her young son as he plays with the water hose in the front yard (77–78). Arriving home, Roy finds Paul preparing to go to work, acknowledging that time off would not help get "everything back to normal" (81). This account of Monday's events resembles other episodes, revealing characters' responses by blending description with actions and dialogue.

Although the people are shocked that a lynching could occur in 1981, they do not passively accept injustice. Having guns in their closets or in their automobiles, speaking out to law enforcement officers, rallying in front of the courthouse where the remnants of the burned cross remain, hacking down the hanging tree in broad daylight, having skilled lawyers continue to pursue legal avenues—most of the citizens of "the city under the trees" remember the painful event but refuse to cower; instead they continue to live their ordinary lives. The one significant exception is Paul Deacon. Having been an enterprising, self-assured youth who "had believed the same faith . . . [his] parents did," his trust in life gave way when he found his friend dangling from the tree on Herndon Avenue. He goes through the motions thereafter, but because he is unable to find closure or come to terms with this random act of violence, he loses his will to live. A blend of varying moods, the novel's overall tone is elegiac but not despairing.

Howard's second novel, *Driving the King* (2015), spans more time and covers more space than the first novel, as Nat Weary, a native of Montgomery, returns home in 1945 after serving in Europe in World War II, intent on proposing to Mattie, the young woman who has waited for him. Because he and Nat King Cole had been childhood friends, Weary wants to propose during a Cole concert being held in a segregated theater. When a group of white men leap onto the stage, aiming to beat Cole to death, Weary jumps from the balcony to the stage, grabs the microphone and begins beating the assailants. He saves Cole's life but is sentenced to ten years in prison for the assault and for starting a riot. The white assailants go unpunished.

Howard has spoken several times about his choice of subject matter and the reasons he shifts the attack from Birmingham to Montgomery and the year from 1956 to 1945, and why he invented Nat Weary to save Nat Cole and, after serving a prison term, to become Cole's chauffeur and bodyguard. In an interview with Sebastian Matthews, Howard said:

> I wanted Nat Weary—his family and his personal history—to be something of a prologue to what happened in 1955. So much of that boycott movement had been simmering for years. He was among the black soldiers who had less freedom than German POW's who came to the U.S. . . . I think there are parallels to showing the early days of a future star. The before and aftermath hold lots of subtext. Nat Weary has to deal with all kinds of aftermaths. . . . I wanted to create someone who was deeply aware of the old and the brand new. (Howard, "The Burden of History")

As noted in *Kirkus Reviews*, "[Weary's] narrative voice—tough, shrewd, barely containing the hurt from public and private injustices—is the novel's finest attribute . . . [but] readers [may] lose their mooring within the novel's time shifting tactics." Other critics have pointed out that Nat Cole's thinly developed character diminishes his significance in the novel. As Howard has said, however, the novel focuses on ordinary people. Weary's association with Cole broadens the scope of the novel and allows for more focus on the Montgomery bus boycott. When Weary drives the restored Packard he formerly drove for the family's taxi company from Montgomery to Los Angeles, he experiences a sense of newness. He is not bound by his mythic identity as the man who "saved Nat King Cole." His 1955 view of the California city reveals that it, too, is segregated but offers a more wide-ranging African American community, blending a variety of people, nightclubs, and opportunities to meet women.

As chauffeur and bodyguard, Weary becomes part of Nat King Cole's entourage. He helps sort and open fan mail, making sure no razor blades or other sharp instruments intended to harm Cole arrive with it. He watches as Cole's associates create the setting for the singer's self-financed television program. Although his records are selling well and his voice is known to millions, Nat Cole does not gain a sponsor, and the television show is canceled after a short run.

In both Montgomery and Los Angeles, women play a significant role in the novel, as they take part in the civil rights movement by promoting the bus boycott and participating in the demonstrations. Howard indicates that many avatars of Rosa Parks helped bring about change. Mattie, Weary's former fiancée, is among these active women. While his visit with her is a painful reminder of what could have been, he is impressed by her dedication to the cause and to her family, and he is able to let go of their personal history. He discovers that he is able to risk love again when he is attracted to a woman in California. His communication by telephone with his sister, Marie, keeps him aware of the movement's progress and of family news. When he meets Almena Lomax, an editor for the *Tribune*, he learns that she writes and speaks in support of the boycott and maintains Alabama connections. Smoothly introducing the journalist-editor just as Weary learns of Rosa Parks's arrest, Howard shifts to Nat's sister, Marie, to link ordinary characters with well-known participants in the civil rights struggle. She tells her brother, "We told everybody to stop riding tomorrow." Warned by Nat to be careful, she responds, "I'm more relieved than anything. Been planning for a while and now it's here. . . . Too late to be careful. . . . Been tiptoeing around this sorry town all these years and got squat to show for it" (187).

While less prominent than the boycott and Nat's regeneration, the plot hinges on the secret plan to have Nat King Cole return to Montgomery and give a concert in a predominately Black theater, ten years after the attack on his life. Although such a return never happened, historically, Howard builds on the possibility as Weary and others carry out plans to keep Cole safe in Montgomery. This plot element makes a fitting climax, for Cole is heading to Europe, Weary has found love and a new life in Los Angeles, and the concert symbolizes a momentary transcendence of injustice and suffering through music.

As he stands backstage, observing the successful return of Nat King Cole, Weary thinks, "I had reached the place where I looked forward more than back. I looked forward to the horn solos, the long held notes" (320). He further describes his satisfaction in this moment: "I watched people listening. . . . I needed to see it, that look on their faces when that moment began. The waiting was behind them, because we had brought our people the show they had imagined for so very long" (321).

Howard's respect for the power of language, akin to music, he believes, has led him to create characters, situations, and settings that honor the ordinary citizens of African American communities and reveal historical events as complexly layered experiences. Revelation through fact and fiction can be a form of protest. Howard concludes his essay "Elevator Music" by asserting that his form of protest is to boycott any business, organization, or place that fails to treat African Americans with respect (163). In the manner of Thoreau, he acts as a "majority of one." As a novelist, Howard creates realistic characters, scenes, and episodes in a prose style that evokes responses and offers insights for readers of diverse identities and backgrounds.

Works Cited

Howard, Ravi. ". . . And Mourning Jubilee." *New York Times*, May 29, 2010. https://www
.nytimes.com/2010/05/30/opinion/30Howard.html. Accessed November 3, 2018.

Howard, Ravi. "The Burden of History: An Interview with Ravi Howard." Interview with Sebastian Matthews. *Fiction Writers Review*, June 15, 2015. https://fictionwritersreview.com
/interview/the-burden-of-history-an-interview-with-ravi-howard. Accessed November 3, 2018.

Howard, Ravi. *Driving the King*. HarperCollins, 2015.

Howard, Ravi. "*Driving the King*: A Story Long in the Works." Interview with Arun Rath. NPR, January 24, 2015. https://www.npr.org/2015/01/24/379632112/driving-the-king-a-story-long
-in-the-works. Accessed November 3, 2018.

Howard, Ravi. "Elevator Music." In *Children of the Changing South: Accounts of Growing Up during and after Integration*, edited by Foster Dickson, 161–63. McFarland, 2011.

Howard, Ravi. "In Conversation with Ravi Howard." Interview with Tayari Jones. *Salon*, January 27, 2015. https://www.salon.com/2015/01/27/ravi_howard_on_singer_nat_king
_cole_the_jackie_robinson_of_television. Accessed November 3, 2018.

Howard, Ravi. *Like Trees, Walking*. HarperCollins, 2007.

Howard, Ravi. "Novelist Ravi Howard on 'Like Trees, Walking.'" Interview with Michel Martin. NPR, March 7, 2007. https://www.npr.org/templates/story/story.php?storyId=7754928. Accessed November 3, 2018.

Howard, Ravi. "The Sunday *Rumpus* Interview: Ravi Howard." Interview with Amina Gautier. *The Rumpus*, February 7, 2016. https://therumpus.net/2016/02/the-Sunday-rumpus-interview
-ravi-howard. Accessed November 3, 2018.

Maslin, Janet. "On the Civil Rights Map, a Crooner and His Driver." *New York Times*, December 28, 2014. https://www.nytimes.com/2014/12/29/arts/in-driving-the-king-ravi
-howard-imagines-nat-king-cole.html. Accessed November 3, 2018.

"Review of *Driving the King*." *Kirkus Reviews*, January 6, 2015. https://www.kirkusreviews.com
/book-reviews/ravi-howard/driving-the-king. Accessed November 3, 2018.

Skip Horack is a native of Louisiana and a graduate of Florida State University. After practicing law in Baton Rouge for five years, he was a Jones Lecturer and a Wallace Stegner Fellow at Stanford. His short story collection *The Southern Cross* was awarded the Bread Loaf Writers' Conference Bakeless Prize in 2008 and was published by Mariner Books in 2009. His debut novel, *The Eden Hunter*, was published by Counterpoint in 2010, and HarperCollins released his second novel, *The Other Joseph*, in 2015. He is currently an assistant professor of English at Florida State University.

Skip Horack
Representing the People

Phillip Howerton

Skip Horack's work has been widely and positively reviewed, and reviewers have noted several consistencies running through his fiction. His work is grounded in the South, he displays great empathy for his characters, and his protagonists are survivors struggling to make a better life for themselves. Such consistencies, however, do not make his work easy to categorize. Although his fiction has southern settings and engages themes associated with genres of southern writing, Horack delivers a broad range of characters, experiences, and perspectives, complicating any attempt to pigeonhole him as a regionalist or to relegate his work to a subgenre. In addition, he refuses to indulge in any easy constructions of place and culture and instead focuses on life as it is lived by his characters, allowing them to authenticate themselves and to illustrate the evolving complexity of the region.

The twelve stories in *The Southern Cross* set the tone of Horack's work, for they deliver a diversity of southern settings, themes, and characters and appeal to readers inside and outside the region. In an interview in the *Southeast Review*, Horack noted that these stories are set in places he knows through deep experience: "I find that if I think hard enough on a particular dot on that Gulf Coast map a story will eventually come to me" ("The Southern Cross: Skip Horack"). This regional knowledge grew out of his upbringing in Louisiana and his early career as young attorney specializing in health-care law. He points out that his firm's "primary clients were hospitals throughout Louisiana" and that he "spent a lot of time on the road, visiting small towns in every part of the state and speaking with all sorts of interesting people" ("The Southern Cross: Skip Horack"). His duty was to listen to, rather than judge, these clients, and Horack is always in his protagonists' corner, representing them and believing in them. Such authenticity and empathy are an endearing combination, and *The Southern Cross* garnered the 2008 Bread Loaf Writers' Conference Bakeless Prize and was praised by numerous critics and writers. For example, the *Boston Globe* commented that the book is an "engrossing collection of short stories . . . about the characters who inhabit them, easily and profoundly," and Rick Bass commented, "These stories are the real deal. . . . They move at depth with what can only be called a great and authentic soul."

The Southern Cross does not fit comfortably into the categories of Grit Lit and Rough South, but numerous aspects of these rowdy genres emerge in the stories. Brian Carpenter describes Grit Lit as "typically blue collar or working class, mostly small town, sometimes rural, occasionally but not always violent," and Rough South as "mostly poor, white, rural, and unquestionably violent" ("Introduction: Blood and Bone," xxvii). Horack's protagonists live or work in a rural community or small town, but they are not limited to any race or class and are rarely violent. They are a variety of ages, ranging from a high school senior to a strong-willed, elderly widow living in a senior center; they are male and female and Black, white, and Mexican; and they range in occupation from dockworker to stripper to poet to attorney. Though diverse by almost any measure, none indulge in or celebrate physical violence. Only two instances of violence appear: in "The Redfish," an accidental death during an arranged bare-knuckle fight is related through the memory of the protagonist; and in "Borderlands," a reflexive act of fear prompts a young hunter to shoot a murderer burying a victim in the woods—and both of these protagonists question the morality of their actions.

Elements of noir are inherent in these stories, as Horack's characters live in bleak surroundings and develop a heightened but healthy cynicism. Horack is especially apt at supplying expressionistic details to suggest the milieu. The setting of "Chores" is a "singlewide trailer" in "foot tall" grass (18); the protagonist in "The Journeyman" lives next to a vacant lot of "shattered glass and ragweed" (20); a paraplegic veteran lives in a "trashy apartment complex stuck between railroad tracks and the highway," which suggests the mobility of the world surrounding him (126). In addition, several protagonists face diverse personal challenges, such as having a mentally handicapped child dying of a bad heart, being convicted of a murder that someone else committed, the death of a spouse, a parent with Alzheimer's. Considering the environments in which they live and the unfairness they endure, these characters must be respected for their responses to these realities. None are self-perpetuating victims or nihilists, and their experiences have enhanced their empathy for others, for they know how it feels to hurt.

As with elements of the Rough South and noir, so historical issues are a natural part of the background in *The Southern Cross*. Although these issues do not rule the characters' lives, they foreshadow and shadow their futures. The book is divided into four seasonal parts, and each part's tone and themes parallel the evolution of Hurricane Katrina. The spring stories carry a sense of approaching crises; each story in the summer part centers on the climax of a crisis; the fall stories focus on the immediate aftermath; and the winter stories suggest the protagonists' futures. In the opening story, "The Caught Fox," a young father realizes that his reckless habits are destroying his relationship with his ex-wife and dying son. In "The Redfish," the last story in the summer part, the protagonist survives Katina but ponders his moral guilt when he fails to save a woman who did not want to be saved. In the fall part, the protagonist of "Little Man" attempts to maintain the family honey farm and care for his father, who has Alzheimer's. In "Visual of a Sparrow," a protagonist made homeless and destitute by Katrina attempts to build a new life, but racism and classism threaten this new self.

Horack depicts the South he knows rather than a mythical place, and two quintessential American themes arise in these stories: the diminished sense of self and the diminished sense of place. Several of the protagonists suffer the emotional or physical loss of a loved one and then question their own purpose and place in society. For instance, the protagonist in "The High Place I Go" is a nurse in a VA hospital who knows her husband is routinely unfaithful. She decides to end the marriage, and she then allows herself to fall in love with a much younger patient, a paraplegic marine. In "East Texas," the protagonist has been giving his sister-in-law and his young niece steady financial support while his brother serves a twenty-year prison term. Meeting his sister-in-law at a roadside café, he gives her "the five twenties that were folded in the front pocket of his work shirt" as he gently suggests that she should visit the prison, but she counters that her "job in life is to raise that little girl" and his brother "poisons everything he touches" (177, 178). A few minutes later, when the niece locks herself in the bathroom in a fit of frustration, he kicks the stubborn jukebox that stole her dollar, chooses "the first of three songs that he thought might just sound good together," and perhaps realizes that he must invest less in his brother and more in his sister-in-law and niece (178). All the protagonists in the collection, rather than turning to the rough life of alcohol, drugs, and violence, seek to make life better for themselves and, in many cases, for those within their sphere of influence.

In his first novel, *The Eden Hunter*, Horack reaches back more than two centuries to the extremely rough South of the late 1700s and early 1800s. Although distant in time, this setting is filled with beginnings that would evolve into key elements of today's Rough South literature, such as an ill-fated protagonist, ubiquitous violence, and racial divides. Horack again complicates any easy categorization, for his protagonist is far removed from the typical Rough South character. Kau is a Pygmy African who has been sold into slavery after the destruction of his village and the massacre of his people. He is a slave to a Georgia innkeeper for five years before escaping into the frontiers of Georgia and Florida to search for his own Eden, a small place apart where he will be free to remember his people and to worship his pagan god. During his escape, he accidently kills the young son of the innkeeper and is hunted by slave catchers and militia. Even when he is beyond the reach of his master, most everyone Kau encounters, whether white, Native, or Black, tries to own him and to enlist him in their hopeless attempts to resist the cultural upheaval engulfing them.

If described as "unquestionably violent," *The Eden Hunter* epitomizes the Rough South, for Kau's native world is destroyed by violence, he is violently removed to a new world, and his odyssey in search of Eden is fraught with violence. This early South is an Eden made vicious and chaotic by the displacements and destruction wrought by the expansion of the United States. This world is filled with the most desperate and vengeful violence imaginable, as an assortment of people, including white settlers, slaves and escaped slaves, American soldiers, and fragments of Native American tribes, ferociously pursue their competing visions of the future. Many have nothing left except a desire for revenge, and in this vicious cycle of viciousness, the only governing principle is to be more brutal than any enemy. The legacy and history of the South grew from this beginning, and Horack's depiction of this distant past foreshadows the brutal future of Indian removal, the growth of slavery, civil war, and Jim Crow, in which almost everyone is reduced to either predator or prey.

Like the protagonists in *The Southern Cross*, Kau survives his desperate circumstances by developing a healthy cynicism. In both of his worlds, he witnesses the cruelty of every civilization and tribe he encounters, acknowledges his own participation in these evils, and is at times nearly overwhelmed by hopelessness, anger, and guilt. During one especially desperate episode, he is almost overwhelmed by these feelings. However, he wards off self-destructive cynicism by proving he has the courage to free himself through death: "Kau pressed the tip of his knife against his bare chest and was not afraid. There was comfort for him there, knowing he had that one power still—the only absolute power that any man ever truly possesses" (77). This knowledge allows him to continue living, for he is devoted to remembering his people and praising his god until his death, and he knows that he has the power to end his life when he is no longer able to carry out those duties.

Of Horack's three books, *The Eden Hunter* most deliberately engages historical events, as he places the novel at the intersection of three central forces giving birth to the American South: the creation of a federal government, the eradication of Native peoples, and the enslavement of Africans. The opening words of his prologue bring these worlds together: "Central Africa, 1786." This phrase introduces two disparate worlds—the remote African jungles and the newly created United States—and places them on an unlikely but inevitable collision course as the new federalism transforms thirteen colonies into a nation profiting from the displacement of other peoples. The American dream, which has brought multitudes to these shores, entails the establishment of a personal Eden and the dream of a future Eden—or the nightmare of a lost Eden. The quest motivates and haunts almost every character. This search for Eden provides the foundation for several other American themes that Horack explores throughout the novel, such as the effort to rise socially and morally, unstable social structures, the destruction of wilderness, and the tradition of violence.

The Other Joseph is set about as far south as one can go in the continental United States—on an offshore oil rig in the Gulf of Mexico. As in Horack's two preceding books, much of the Rough South lurks in the background. Although the protagonist, Roy Joseph, was brought up middle-class, he quickly finds himself on the gritty side of the working class. His parents were schoolteachers who owned a small farm, but they never recovered emotionally after his older brother, a Navy SEAL, went missing in action during Desert Storm. Roy's parents died in a car accident six years later, and shortly after their deaths, at nineteen Roy was convicted for having sex with a sixteen-year-old girl. He then sold the small family farm and moved downstate to avoid public scandal, locked the insurance and real estate monies in investments, and began working on an oil rig. He plans to retire at thirty, when he will no longer be listed as a sex offender, and then to draw out his estimated two million in savings to live any life he imagines. Until that time, though, he plans to remain a loner, but when he is contacted by a teenage girl in California who claims to be the daughter of his brother, he undertakes a cross-country odyssey in search of family.

Once again, Horack and his protagonist resist the Rough South, for although Roy appears to be living the rough life, he refuses to embrace that world. He still drives the car his parents gave him when he was sixteen, and he works steadily at a rough blue-collar job, but he has remained unmarried and lives in a trailer on a rented lot. He also avoids the violence of the Rough South. Although Roy participates in situations that would typically prompt violence in Rough South literature, such as having a variety of tough coworkers, occasionally visiting a bar, traveling across the United States in a junk car, and using a Russian dating service, he engages in no loud and heated exchanges, no drunken tempests, and no physical brawls. Indeed, in several situations when he might rightfully be angry, he displays empathy for others and converts a potentially violent scene into a moment of healing. For example, when Roy goes on an expensive arranged date with a potential wife-to-be, the Russian nanny admits that she is in love with a man back in her home country; however, rather than starting a shouting match, Roy listens to her story and advises her. She closes the conversation by saying, "You are a good man. A much better man than I thought you would be" (208).

Although Desert Storm provides the novel's context, the focus remains on Roy's cross-country odyssey, so there is no shortage of American themes. Roy goes west to California in search of the past and in search of family. He occasionally allows himself to indulge in a moment of fantasy about the new life he might achieve. One version of his imaginings has him living in a small town on the Gulf Coast in a house like those featured in *Southern Living*, worshipping "at a United Methodist," married to a "big-haired, bless-her-hearting girl," taking vacations, going hunting and fishing, and volunteering in the community (213–14). This version of the future contains standard elements of the American dream, such as "layers and layers of family, friends, and possessions" (214). In another version, he is a romantic loner who has "no one to please or be accountable for" and spends his "days traveling, getting into adventures, seeing the world," and letting his hair grow long (214). Based on his past experiences, however, Roy remains realistic and wryly cynical about the future, as is suggested by his encounter with a Google car at a rest area early in his trip west. Roy notes that the car's cameras are "ready to tame everything. To continue shrinking the world even as [he is] trying to explore it" (85). He recognizes that his probable future will be a road well traveled by numerous others whose lives are as nondescript, existentially bankrupt, and regimented as the life of the Google car driver, whom he describes as "a chinless, balding man wearing khakis and a lime-green polo," whose "backseat [is] buried under crumpled fast-food bags and popped cans of Red Bull" (85–86).

Horack is difficult to press into a specific category or subgenre, so perhaps it is best to recognize him as an extremely gifted and insightful American author grounded in a place he truly knows. He presents this region in a complex and informed manner, refusing to sacrifice his characters to preconceived cultural expectations. He shows that life in the South is infinitely complex, more than a simple division between rough and genteel or the two sides of a railroad track. Because he allows his characters to maintain their humanity, he is able to render authentic depictions of the South while connecting life there to universal experiences and themes. Simply put, Horack is the type of writer all regions need: a writer who thoroughly knows and deeply loves a place and believes that the people who live there have worth and should be empowered to improve their lives and the lives of others.

Works Cited

Bass, Rick. "Praise." Comment on Skip Horack. http://skiphorack.com/praise.
Birkerts, Sven. "Lost in America." *New York Times Sunday Book Review*, October 8, 2010. https://www.nytimes.com/2010/10/10/books/review/Birkerts-t.html. Accessed September 27, 2018.
Carpenter, Brian. "Introduction: Blood and Bone." In *Grit Lit: A Rough South Reader*, edited by Brian Carpenter and Tom Franklin, xiii–xxxii. University of South Carolina Press, 2012.

Heller, Amanda. "Short Takes." *Boston Globe*, September 6, 2009. Boston.com. http://archive
.boston.com/ae/books/articles/2009/09/06/short_takes_boston_globe. Accessed
September 27, 2018.

Horack, Skip. *The Eden Hunter*. Mariner, 2009.

Horack, Skip. *The Other Joseph*. Ecco, 2015.

Horack, Skip. *The Southern Cross*. Counterpoint, 2010.

Horack, Skip. "The Southern Cross: Skip Horack on His Award-Winning, Debut Collection."
Interview with Jessica Pitchford. *Southeast Review*, September 18, 2009. https://southeastrev
.org/2009/-9/skip-horack.html. Accessed September 27, 2018.

Jesmyn Ward was born in Oakland, California, in 1977 but grew up in rural DeLisle on Mississippi's Gulf Coast. She received her MFA from the University of Michigan and has received the MacArthur Fellowship, a Stegner Fellowship, a John and Renée Grisham Writers Residency, and the Strauss Living Prize. She is the winner of two National Book Awards for Fiction for *Sing, Unburied, Sing* (2017) and *Salvage the Bones* (2011). She is also the author of the novel *Where the Line Bleeds* (2008) and the memoir *Men We Reaped* (2013), which was a finalist for the National Book Critics Circle Award and won the Chicago Tribune Heartland Prize and the Media for a Just Society Award. She also edited the essay anthology *The Fire This Time* (2016). In 2020 she published the text of her 2018 commencement address at Tulane University, titled *Navigate Your Stars*, with illustration by Gina Triplet. Ward is an associate professor of creative writing at Tulane University and lives in Mississippi.

Songs for the Unsung

Jesmyn Ward's Narratives of Race, Loss, and Survival

Joan Wylie Hall

The characters of Jesmyn Ward's fictional Bois Sauvage, Mississippi, were inspired by the impoverished Black community of her youth. She says, "I love the idea that my work is part of the Dirty South" ("Literary Voice of the Dirty South," 267). She appreciates the "rawness" of the genre: "A certain honesty. A willingness to bring secrets and despair and hope and all those other messy human emotions to life." Generations of poverty and other challenges to survival in the Dirty South have inspired courage "born of desperation," and Ward believes "women can speak to those issues just as well as men. The hardships of this life don't discriminate by gender" (268). In the final chapter of her memoir *Men We Reaped* (2013), Ward cites statistics for "what it means to be Black and poor in the South" (236). "By the numbers, by all of the official records," she concludes, "here at the confluence of history, of racism, of poverty, and economic power, this is what our lives are worth: nothing" (237). Reflecting on the sudden deaths, between 2000 and 2004, of her brother and four other young Black men from her small community, Ward describes the impact on survivors: "We drank too much, smoked too much, were abusive to ourselves, to each other. We were bewildered. There is a great darkness bearing down on our lives, and no one acknowledges it" (249–50). Jesmyn Ward's depictions of the rough South acknowledge the darkness while also asserting the incalculable worth of each imperiled life.

After the publication of her first novel, *Where the Line Bleeds* (2008), Ward told the interviewer Brad Hooper that "her close relationship with her brother and the close-knit community she grew up in provided her with her major theme—making your own way in the world" (Ward, "Jesmyn Ward's *Where the Line Bleeds*, 28). Named after Ward's hometown of DeLisle, the protagonists are eighteen-year-old twins who have always shared a strong bond, but they take drastically different paths the summer they graduate in the class of 2005. An epigraph from the book of Genesis foretells this divergence by describing the fighting of Rebekah's twins, Jacob and Esau, even in the womb. While Joshua DeLisle is hired for heavy physical labor at the coastal dockyard, his brother Christophe's application is rejected: "The hurt and love and jealousy in Christophe's chest coalesced and turned to annoyance that bubbled from his throat" (*Where the Line Bleeds*, 48). In one of Ward's frequent time-shifts, Christophe remembers "playing chase" in competition with other children. The twins' team typically won because of the brothers' complementary skills: "Christophe was the fastest, so he led Joshua in a general direction, but Joshua always had the better eye for hiding spots" (50). The two would stay hidden for hours, finally running home "drunk with their cleverness, wrestling each other down the length of the road" (51).

At eighteen, however, Christophe fears "he would have to find his way alone" (*Where the Line Bleeds*, 51). When he fails to land even a fast-food position, a cousin encourages him to sell marijuana; the choice upsets Joshua, although both brothers smoke weed from the start of the novel. After their estranged father, Sandman, returns to Bois Sauvage and relapses into drug addiction, a fight breaks out at the house of Javon, a cocaine dealer who supervises Christophe's growing marijuana sales. The twins find themselves on opposite sides: "Wet, teary, they wrestled face to face" (224). With blood from his father, his brother, and himself on his shirt, Joshua rushes Christophe to the emergency room with a deep stab wound inflicted by Sandman. "I tried to save him" (229), the distraught Joshua tells their widowed grandmother, Ma-mee, who had begged him to protect his twin. Christophe survives the stabbing, but bloodshed and bloodlines are sources of sorrow throughout *Where the Line Bleeds*; the twins' relationship with their parents is especially strained. Their mother, Cille, has worked in Atlanta since the boys were five, and her visits back to Ma-mee's home in Bois Sauvage are rare.

Despite the strength of their love for one another, Ma-mee and her grandsons seem to be heading toward disaster as the summer passes. Diabetic and nearly blind after forty years of cleaning white people's houses, Ma-mee mourns the changes in the community, from the loss of the creole French language of her youth to "the crackheads and drugs that seemed to steal the sense from people" (*Where the Line Bleeds*, 64). She feels "a shadow passing over her, a scuttling cloud obscuring her from the sun of life" (65). Nature is generally beneficent in *Where the Line Bleeds*: at the beginning, the twins dive into the river on their May graduation day; at the end, they fish in the bayou in August. Yet Christophe's alienation in the middle chapters makes Joshua long for an evening rain "to become a biblical flood so that it would not only wash him through space, but through time"—back to the rainy day when the seven-year-old twins seemed to "run forever" (129), hand in hand. Joshua's imagery is equally apocalyptic in mid-July when the twins drive to the New Orleans airport to meet Cille: "The whole city seemed on the verge of collapsing, of coming apart and spewing into the streets to slide and submerge in the river. Joshua imagined it all gone: the levees, the sea of white aboveground tombs, the French Quarter" (166). Although Hurricane Katrina is never mentioned in the novel, Ma-mee's TV has forecast that a large storm is building in the Gulf. The idyllic fishing scene that closes the book takes place a week or two before landfall.

In the twelve-day span of Ward's second novel, *Salvage the Bones* (2011), the storm approaches Bois Sauvage, then strikes disastrously. The DeLisle twins are mentioned in passing, but Ward's new focus is the Batistes, another family from the community, and the narrative voice this time is not third-person but first-person and female. According to the NPR interviewer Melissa Block, "Reading was [an] escape" for Jesmyn Ward as a child, "especially books about spunky girls" (Ward, "Writing of Mississippi"); but Ward never encountered Black girls in books like Astrid Lindgren's *Pippi Longstocking*. The pregnant fifteen-year-old protagonist of Ward's National Book Award–winning novel is as spirited as any of the strong white characters in young adult fiction. In fact, the reviewer Andy Johnson suggests that Esch Batiste "embodies the classical hero. She is protector and defender, of herself, of her brothers and father, of her unborn child, and the memory of her mother" (493).

Classical precedent is surprisingly apt for Esch, who often draws on Edith Hamilton's *Mythology*, the book her high school English teacher assigned for summer reading. Mythic women, says Esch, "kept me turning the pages:

the trickster nymphs, the ruthless goddesses, the world-uprooting mothers" (*Salvage the Bones*, 15). In her narrative of two dramatic weeks in August 2005, the motherless teenager mentions several female legends, from Artemis to Psyche; but she refers most frequently to Medea. Medea's story is Esch's subtext in the novel's final section, where she pictures the treacherous Katrina as "the mother that swept into the Gulf and slaughtered. Her chariot was a storm so great and black the Greeks would say it was harnessed to dragons" (255). Albeit a "murderous mother who cut us to the bone," Katrina nevertheless "left us alive" and "left us to salvage" (255). Benjamin Eldon Stevens suggests that Esch's fascination with the sorceress-lover is "a way of understanding her own experience as a young woman coming of age, entering motherhood and confronting the responsibilities it entails, and more generally responding to forces—in her body, in her community, and in nature—that are beyond her control but nonetheless let her show an impressive power" (158).

Sinéad Moynihan explores similar parallels between Ward's protagonist and the central women in William Faulkner's *As I Lay Dying*, Esch's English text for the previous summer. Like Esch, for example, Faulkner's Addie Bundren and her teenage daughter Dewey Dell cope with sexual crises, family conflicts, and rising waters. Moynihan, however, demonstrates that *Salvage the Bones* is much more than a rewriting of Faulkner's epic novel. Instead Jesmyn Ward "engages in a new form of re-visionary fiction that engages more emphatically than previous models of rewriting in a critique of contemporary sociopolitical realities" (Moynihan, "From Disposability to Recycling," 566). Thus Laura Fine argues that "Ward portrays an African American rural community devastated not only by Hurricane Katrina, but by popular culture's misconceptions and misrepresentations of it" ("Make Them Know," 49). At the same time, as Christopher W. Clark stresses, "In the face of abandonment and left to waste, the characters of *Salvage the Bones* band together in solidarity, challenging the expected outcome of black bodies left to perish in the South" ("What Comes to the Surface," 357). Interviewed by Lisa Allardice, Ward says she aimed to "give voice" to teenagers like Esch because they are "silenced, they are misunderstood, and they are underestimated. Black girls period: pregnant young black girls, poor black girls—girls like that are diminished in American culture" (Ward, "Jesmyn Ward: 'Black Girls'").

When Katrina passes, Esch realizes that she, her brothers, and their father are "all bleeding, all gashed" (*Salvage the Bones*, 239); likewise, "the trees I had known, the oaks in the bend, the stand of pines on the long stretch, the magnolia at the four-way, were all broken, all crumbled" (241–42). Paula Gallant Eckard contrasts Ward's novel to many southern childhood narratives because *Salvage the Bones* views life as "passionate and harsh, exacting and raw" ("Lost Childhood in Southern Literature," 87). Still, Esch perseveres, even after she is deserted by Manny, the boyfriend she compares to Medea's fickle lover Jason. When Randall, her oldest brother, threatens to "beat the shit out of him," Esch says, "You don't need to. I already did" (*Salvage the Bones*, 244). Her loyal friend Big Henry counters Manny's betrayal by assuring her that her baby will have "plenty daddies" (255). Prominent among these faithful young men is her closest brother, Skeetah, who released his grasp on his beloved dog, China, to grab Esch from the engulfing flood. She envisions their seven-year-old brother, Junior, feeding her baby, just as she fed the infant Junior after their mother died in childbirth. Even their father, who drinks and treats the siblings harshly in several earlier scenes, shows a gentle side during the storm. He apologizes to Esch for belatedly realizing she is a few months pregnant and says they should seek medical help to "make sure everything's okay. . . . So nothing will go wrong" (247). In an essay on her hometown, Jesmyn Ward describes just how often things go wrong for Black Mississippians who—lacking the resources for adequate health care— are "marked by the neglect of [their] mothers' pregnant health" ("DeLisle, Mississippi"). More hopefully, she told the interviewer Anna Hartwell that *Salvage the Bones* affirms that there are "new possibilities that can be, that can manifest" ("When Cars Become Churches," 216).

Although Ward says she always likes to "at least leave the reader with something to hang on to" ("When Cars Become Churches," 216), she acknowledges how difficult this was for her next book, *Men We Reaped: A Memoir*. The title evokes Harriet Tubman's description of the deaths of Black Union soldiers in an attack on Fort Wagner, South Carolina, during the Civil War. Tubman's extended metaphor for the storm of battle comprises Ward's first epigraph: "We saw the lightning and that was the guns; and then we heard the thunder and that was the big guns; and then we heard the rain falling and that was the blood falling; and when we came to get in the crops, it was dead men that we reaped" (*Men We Reaped*, iii). The rapper Tupac Shakur's "Words 2 My Firstborn" provides a second epigraph, bringing the battle home to DeLisle, Mississippi, where Ward's brother and four other young men, like the adolescents in Shakur's song, died before they could grow. Much as she paired epigraphs from the Bible and the rapper Pastor

Troy for her first novel, Ward parallels passages by Shakur, Harriet Tubman, and the poet A. R. Ammons to "add a certain leg.timacy" to a form of music that is, she says, "lyrically" significant in treating "real issues that should be taken seriously" ("Getting the South Right").

Structurally inventive, her memoir alternates six chapters on the history of Ward's community and family with five chapters on the individual men she memorializes. The historical chapters move forward in time, starting with DeLisle's distant past as Wolf Town and proceeding to the present century, when factory jobs have disappeared from the Gulf Coast and work is scarce, even in the low-paying service industries. The elegiac sequence begins with her friend Roger Eric Daniels III, who died in June 2004 of a heart attack at twenty-three, just a few months after a large dose of cocaine almost killed him. In the last of the five elegies, Ward's nineteen-year-old brother, Joshua Adam Dedeaux, was killed in October 2000 by a drunk driver. Sentenced to five years for leaving an accident scene, the convicted man, who was white, served only three years and never paid the mandated restitution. "This is where the past and the future meet," says Ward of her most painful chapter: "This is the heart. This is. Every day, this is" (*Men We Reaped*, 213). Completing the memoir thirteen years after her brother's death, she believes that her lasting grief, "for all its awful weight, insists that he matters. What we carry of Roger and Demond and C. J. and Ronald says that they matter" (243). Richard Torres observes that Ward "humanizes instead of canonizes," portraying her loved ones' weaknesses along with their strengths and talents.

The reviewer Dominique Nicole Swann adds that Ward "successfully reveals how an epidemic of racism and economic inequality has affected and continues to haunt her family and her community. But her reflections gesture at an epidemic that reaches far beyond the Gulf Coast" (79). In editing *The Fire This Time: A New Generation Speaks about Race* (2016), Ward looks more searchingly at the scope of the epidemic. Inspired by the death of Trayvon Martin, to whom the book is dedicated, she "needed words" that were more permanent than the emotions expressed on Black Twitter (*The Fire This Time*, 6)—words like James Baldwin's "brutally honest" scrutiny of racism in *The Fire Next Time* (1963). Writing for the *New York Times*, Jamil Smith says that Natasha Trethewey, Kiese Laymon, Claudia Rankine, and their fellow poets and essayists in Ward's anthology are all "grounded in a harsh reality that our nation, at large, refuses fully to confront. In the spirit of Baldwin's centering of black experiences, they force everyone to see things our way."

Ward continues to address harsh realities in *Sing, Unburied, Sing* (2017), her second novel to win a National Book Award. Ward told the interviewer Sarah Begley that she "wanted to understand" how Jojo, the first of her three narrators, "would navigate something of a coming of age in the modern South, where, yes, it is modern, but there are multiple waves of the past here" (Ward, "Jesmyn Ward, Heir to Faulkner"). With his father incarcerated on a drug charge and his mother often incapacitated by addiction, thirteen-year-old Jojo gently shelters his three-year-old sister from their parents' neglect. Kayla and Jojo are raised lovingly by Pop and Mam, their elderly maternal grandparents, who have special gifts of protection and healing, just as Jojo has the ability to understand the thoughts of animals and many humans. In one tense scene, the gris-gris bag Pop makes for Jojo helps to save the children from the threat of police brutality. But their paternal grandfather is a white racist who accepts neither his biracial grandchildren nor his son Michael's love for the African American Leonie. In an essay for *The Guardian*, Ward blames the slavery and segregation of earlier generations for the persistent fact that "black children are not granted childhoods" ("Raising a Black Son in the US").

Dramatically, Ward embodies the racial crimes of the past in two ghosts of young Black men who died violently long before the contemporary action of *Sing, Unburied, Sing*. This supernatural element is new to Ward's fiction, and the reviewer Ron Charles suggests that "readers may be reminded of the trapped spirits in George Saunders's recent novel, 'Lincoln in the Bardo,' but Toni Morrison's 'Beloved' is a more direct antecedent." Vinson Cunningham compares the "portentous sentence rhythms" of Morrison and Ward, observing that such prose is "the sign of the seriousness of Ward's subject, and of the trauma through which her characters have passed and will, inevitably, pass again." The first of Ward's trapped spirits is Leonie's dead brother, Given, murdered at eighteen by an older white man during a hunting party. As the novel's second narrator, Leonie describes the hauntings that occur each time Given tries to prevent her from overdosing on drugs, even fifteen years after his death. When Leonie snorts cocaine in her friend Misty's Katrina cottage, the ghost of Given reaches his "big-knuckled, slim-boned hand, toward mine. Like he wanted to support me. . . . Like he could grab my hand and lead me out of there. Like we could go home" (36).

But Leonie doesn't feel at home in her parents' house. At nine, Jojo quits calling her Mama after he has a serious accident the first time she leaves him home alone for hours. Pop no longer addresses her with an affectionate "girl," and Mam believes that Leonie's "love for herself and her love for Michael— well, it gets in the way" of her love for the children (234). When Leonie, Jojo, and Kayla bring Michael back to Bois Sauvage from Parchman prison at the end of his sentence, the couple stays home only two days a week. However, Leonie unexpectedly helps to guide her mother to the afterlife by gathering an altar of stones in Mam's bedroom and reciting a sacred litany to Maman Brigitte, "mistress of the cemetery and mother of all the dead" (268). Beneath the painted ceiling of constellations, the ghost of Given announces, "I come with the boat, Mama," and Mam Philomène is finally released from the long and bitter pain of cancer as "time floods the room in a storm surge" (269).

Homecoming is equally hard for Richie, a twelve-year-old who died several decades earlier during his desperate escape from the notorious Parchman. Until he conceals himself on the back floor of Leonie's car, his restless spirit remains in the Mississippi Delta, bound to the land where prison dogs mauled his body. In an interview for NPR, Ward credits David Oshinsky's *Worse Than Slavery: Parchman Farm and the Ordeal of Jim Crow Justice* (1997) with teaching her that, early in the twentieth century, young boys were "enslaved and suffered and were tortured and sometimes died in Parchman prison, and their suffering had been erased from history in some ways" ("For Jesmyn Ward, Writing Means Telling"). Ward says she had to make the dead prisoner Richie a ghost, both to give him the "voice" to tell this history as the book's third narrator and also to allow him to interact with living characters ("For Jesmyn Ward"). A climactic encounter occurs in Jojo's closing chapter when the tiny Kayla frees Richie along with a host of other murdered men, women, and children. "Go home," she commands the troubled spirits, and then she sings "a song of mismatched, half-garbled words" that makes them "smile with something like relief, something like remembrance, something like ease" (284). In the novel's final line, Jojo's gift of insight lets him hear their glad response to Kayla's powerful song: "*Home,* they say. *Home*" (285).

Throughout *Sing, Unburied, Sing*, Pop tells family stories to Jojo, including ancestral memories of the Middle Passage from Africa and accounts of American enslavement. Jesmyn Ward's next novel will probe the experience of slavery through the life of a young Black woman in antebellum New Orleans. The new setting is remote in time and place from the Katrina-era fictions of Bois Sauvage, Mississippi. But, as Jonathan Miles observes in reviewing *Sing, Unburied, Sing,* "Ward's essential—and essentially Southern—focus" reveals "how the weight and stain of history affect every one of us" ("Haunting Melody").

Works Cited

Charles, Ron. "Jesmyn Ward's Powerful New Novel, 'Sing, Unburied, Sing.'" Review of *Sing, Unburied, Sing,* by Jesmyn Ward. *Washington Post,* August 29, 2017. https://www .washingtonpost.com. Accessed September 29, 2018.

Clark, Christopher W. "What Comes to the Surface: Storms, Bodies, and Community in Jesmyn Ward's *Salvage the Bones.*" *Mississippi Quarterly* 68, nos. 3–4 (2015): 341–58.

Cunningham, Vinson. "Jesmyn Ward's Haunted Novel of the Gulf Coast." Review of *Sing, Unburied, Sing,* by Jesmyn Ward. *New Yorker,* September 11, 2017. https://www.newyorker .com. Accessed August 10, 2018.

Eckard, Paula Gallant. "Lost Childhood in Southern Literature." *Southern Quarterly* 54, nos. 3–4 (2017): 75–93.

Fine, Laura. "'Make Them Know': Jesmyn Ward's *Salvage the Bones.*" *South Carolina Review* 49, no. 2 (2016): 48–58.

Johnson, Andy. Review of *Salvage the Bones,* by Jesmyn Ward. *Callaloo* 39, no. 2 (2016): 493–95.

Miles, Jonathan. "Haunting Melody: Jesmyn Ward's Latest Novel Expands the Southern Canon." Review of *Sing, Unburied, Sing,* by Jesmyn Ward. *Garden & Gun,* August–September 2017, 50.

Moynihan, Sinéad. "From Disposability to Recycling: William Faulkner and the New Politics of Rewriting in Jesmyn Ward's *Salvage the Bones.*" *Studies in the Novel* 47, no. 4 (2015): 550–67.

Smith, Jamil. "Jesmyn Ward's Anthology of Race Builds on the Legacy of James Baldwin." Review of *The Fire This Time,* edited by Jesmyn Ward. *New York Times,* August 13, 2016. https://www.nytimes.com. Accessed October 16, 2018.

Stevens, Benjamin Eldon. "Medea in Jesmyn Ward's *Salvage the Bones.*" *International Journal of the Classical Tradition* 25, no. 2 (2018): 158–77.

Swann, Dominique Nicole. Review of *Men We Reaped: A Memoir,* by Jesmyn Ward. *World Literature Today* 88, no. 6 (November–December 2014): 78–79.

Torres, Richard. "In 'Reaped,' 5 Lives That Are Far More Than Just Statistics." Review of *Men We Reaped,* by Jesmyn Ward. NPR Books, September 17, 2013. https://www.npr.org. Accessed September 3, 2018.

Ward, Jesmyn. "DeLisle, Mississippi." *Harper's Magazine,* October 2017. https://www.harpers .org. Accessed October 16, 2018.

Ward, Jesmyn, ed. *The Fire This Time: A New Generation Speaks about Race.* Scribner, 2016.

Ward, Jesmyn. "For Jesmyn Ward, Writing Means Telling the 'Truth about the Place That I Live In.'" Interview with Sam Briger. *NPR Fresh Air,* hosted by Terry Gross, November 28, 2017. https://www.npr.org. Accessed August 10, 2018.

Ward, Jesmyn. "Getting the South Right: A Conversation with Jesmyn Ward." Interview with Nico Berry. *Fiction Writers Review,* August 19, 2009. https://www.fictionwritersreview.com. Accessed August 11, 2018.

Ward, Jesmyn. "Introduction." In *The Fire This Time: A New Generation Speaks about Race*, edited by Jesmyn Ward, 3–11. Scribner, 2016.

Ward, Jesmyn. "Jesmyn Ward: 'Black Girls Are Silenced, Misunderstood and Underestimated.'" Interview with Lisa Allardice. *The Guardian*, May 11, 2018. https://www.theguardian.com. Accessed August 11, 2018.

Ward, Jesmyn. "Jesmyn Ward, Heir to Faulkner, Probes the Specter of Race in the South." Interview with Sarah Begley. *Time*, August 24, 2017. https://www.time.com. Accessed August 10, 2018.

Ward, Jesmyn. "Jesmyn Ward's *Where the Line Bleeds*: Finding Your Way." Story Behind the Story. Interview with Brad Hooper. *Booklist*, November 15, 2008, 28.

Ward, Jesmyn. "Literary Voice of the Dirty South: An Interview with Jesmyn Ward." Interview with Danille K. Taylor. *CLA Journal* 60, no. 2 (2016): 266–68.

Ward, Jesmyn. *Men We Reaped: A Memoir*. Bloomsbury, 2013.

Ward, Jesmyn. "Raising a Black Son in the US: 'He Had Never Taken a Breath, and I Was Already Mourning Him.'" *The Guardian*, October 28, 2017. https://www.theguardian.com. Accessed August 11, 2018.

Ward, Jesmyn. *Salvage the Bones*. Bloomsbury, 2011.

Ward, Jesmyn. *Sing, Unburied, Sing*. Scribner, 2017.

Ward, Jesmyn. "When Cars Become Churches: Jesmyn Ward's Disenchanted America; An Interview." Interview with Anna Hartnell. *Journal of American Studies* 50, no. 1 (2016): 205–18.

Ward, Jesmyn. *Where the Line Bleeds*. Agate, 2008.

Ward, Jesmyn. "Writing of Mississippi: Jesmyn Ward Salvages Stories of the Silenced." Interview with Melissa Block. *NPR News*, hosted by Ari Shapiro, August 31, 2017. https://www.npr.org. Accessed August 10, 2018.

Born in Fayetteville, North Carolina, in 1977, and having grown up in Gastonia, North Carolina, **Wiley Cash** proclaims, "That's why I started writing about the South in the first place—to feel at home" ("Many Souths"). Cash's plots and characters place him firmly within the culture of his native state. After receiving a BA in literature from the University of North Carolina Asheville, an MA from the University of North Carolina Greensboro, and a PhD in English and creative writing from the University of Louisiana at Lafayette, Cash settled briefly in West Virginia before returning to Wilmington, North Carolina, where he lives with his family. Cash teaches in the Mountainview Low-Residency MFA Program in Creative Writing at Southern New Hampshire University, serves as writer-in-residence at UNC Asheville, and has been the Appalachian Writer in Residence at Shepherd University in West Virginia. Noting that he thinks "one thing that defines the South broadly and Southern literature in general is the idea of struggle and all the forms it takes" ("Many Souths"), Cash uses southern settings to reveal his musings on universal themes of human relationships, guilt, and redemption.

"Depending on Where You Stop Telling It"
Family and Redemption in the Novels of Wiley Cash

Scott Hamilton Suter

Eighty-seven-year-old Lilly Wiggins concludes Wiley Cash's novel *The Last Ballad* (2017) with a declaration: "There is an old saying that every story, even your own, is either happy or sad depending on where you stop telling it" (370). Her statement applies to many of Cash's characters throughout his three novels, as each text presents the points of view of numerous voices, each recounting his or her own story. Cash acknowledges the influence of Faulkner's multiple-narrator works, and he presents what George Hovis identifies as "an *internal* voice of the character, and one without any explicit auditor, other than the reader" ("Legacy of Thomas Wolfe," 73). These voices tell us each narrator's story, inviting readers to determine whether the accounts are "happy or sad." Close reading reveals that one of Cash's primary themes is the human struggle with loss and feelings of responsibility for others; many of his narrators expose their guilt for actions or inactions that have led to other characters' misery and even death. Their stories reflect a desire for redemption for their self-realized transgressions. Leaving the telling to his characters, Cash also leaves open the possibility of either a happy or sad ending depending, as Lilly Wiggins notes, on when the telling stops. One of the values of reading Cash's novels lies in the opportunity for readers to decide how actions determine the course of not only one's own life but also often the lives of others.

Each of Cash's novels focuses on the importance of family in the lives of his characters, and the quests for redemption in his work frequently revolve around decisions and actions that have led to tragic results for children, siblings, and parents. Examined from this perspective, parent-child relationships drive many of the plots of Cash's novels. Children feature prominently in each work, emphasizing their important roles in the families, and Cash has created realistic adolescents who provide primary character voices in each novel. Jess Hall, Easter Quillby, and Lilly Wiggins offer children's views on their own stories, although Lilly's text comes as a reminiscence late in her life. Strong-willed, creative, intelligent—these children survive the trials of their lives to settle into a fulfilling future.

Jess Hall, the nine-year-old protagonist of *A Land More Kind Than Home* (2012), recounts his experiences with his mute older brother, Christopher (called Stump by others), and his parents, Ben and Julie. Set in Marshall County, North Carolina, during the 1980s, the novel describes a small community in which town elders, including an aging midwife and Sunday school teacher (Adelaide Lyle) and the sheriff (Clem Barefield), feel responsible for the community's members. Jess's story sets up the novel's primary plotline, and it is through his eyes that we see the two events that lead to Stump's death and the novel's complication. On a hot summer Sunday, Jess and his friend Joe Bill are left to roam the riverside, since children have been forbidden to participate in the worship services at the River Road Church of Christ in Signs Following after the death of a member during a snake-handling ritual. On this morning, Adelaide Lyle, who has assumed the role of supervising the children during services, reluctantly allows a church elder to escort Stump to the worship service because, according to the elder, "the Lord's called him" (29). This decision raises a concern for young Jess, who recalls that although his mother told him he was too young to join her in church, "she'd also told me over and over that I should always look out for Stump and make sure that nothing happened to him, that I was like the big brother and he was like the little one" (30). This sense of responsibility, along with needling from Joe Bill, entices Jess to spy through a crack in the church walls to see just what Stump might be experiencing there. The terrifying scene he witnesses shocks him. Pastor Carson Chambliss and another man are lying on top of Stump, and his "feet [are] kicking like he [is] trying to get away" (50). Unable to control himself, Jess shouts out "Mama!" and amid the music and chaos of the laying on of hands, churchgoers believe that Stump has spoken the first word of his life. Jess, knowing that he has disobeyed, says nothing of witnessing the event.

This central action surrounds another, brief, yet even more significant episode involving Jess, Stump, and Pastor Chambliss. As Jess debates spying on the church, he recalls another disturbing eavesdropping event from the previous Friday. The two brothers return home early from a salamander-catching excursion on which their mother had uncharacteristically sent them. As they clean themselves at the water barrel, they hear sounds from their parents' bedroom window, which they recognize are "the same noises that we heard them make in the morning sometimes when they didn't know we were awake yet" (40). Stump's attempt to spy results in the noisy toppling of the rain barrel, but when Jess urges him to run and hide, Stump remains behind. Jess's worry about Stump's spying turns to fear when he sees that the man coming around the corner of the house to investigate the noise is not his father but a shirtless Pastor Chambliss, who simply asks Stump what he saw, laughing when he realizes he won't get a response. From outside, Jess hears Chambliss answer their mother's questioning with a nonchalant response that does not mention Stump.

In this second chapter of the novel, Cash carefully sets up the dilemma faced by his young protagonist. Jess wisely infers that Stump's invitation into the church is related to the boys' witnessing their mother's infidelity with Chambliss, but he is afraid to act on his suspicion. He lies in response to his mother's questions about his actions during church because he realizes that he would also have to tell her that he and Stump have discovered her extramarital affair. Jess eloquently ponders his reaction: "I wished I could go back and stop myself from seeing all the things that I'd seen in the past two days, but I knew there wasn't no way that I could undo any of that now, no matter how bad I wanted to" (59). Jess acknowledges his guilt to Stump as they play that Sunday afternoon after the morning service: "I should have said something to Mama on the way home, and I should've tried to stop them from doing what they did. I shouldn't have let it happen" (73). Later that evening, after a second—this time fatal—laying on of hands, Jess understands that by keeping his secret he contributed to Stump's death. Still, as Cash himself notes, Jess "perceives things but doesn't grasp the full import of them, and that idea of experience and understanding" (quoted in Clark, "Wiley Cash," 67).

Jess does realize that, by telling his story, he might have prevented Stump's death. While playing basketball with Joe Bill, Jess considers telling his friend about what he and Stump witnessed, but he understands that such a revelation would come too late: "I knew that if I was going to tell anybody about that I should've done it before Stump went into the church on Sunday morning, I definitely should've said something before Mama took him back in there that night" (261). Trudging home through a drenching downpour, an experience that Erica Abrams Locklear describes as a "kind of baptism" ("Mountain Fatalism," 121), Jess continues his contemplations and decides to tell his father what he has seen. His confession, an innocent gesture toward redemption, sets off the conflict that will leave Jess fatherless and deserted by his mother.

Hovis describes Jess as a "child who has been emotionally abandoned by his parents whose marital rupture and grief over their son's death occupy all of their attention" (72). Carrying this thought forward, readers see the importance of family in Cash's novel through this absence of family support. This theme carries through into Cash's second novel, as we shall see, but he emphasizes this point in *A Land More Kind Than Home* by introducing the long-absent grandfather Jimmy Hall, who had a negative effect on Jess's father's life. This alcoholic, overbearing father, whose son believed he was capable of killing him for participating in high school shenanigans, returns to his home after many years, hoping to reconcile with his son and grandsons. While Ben Hall, Jess's father, had little family stability, an experience that carries over into his own family, Cash offers a hopeful ending to the story of Jess and Jimmy Hall. After the murder of Stump and a violent and deadly shootout between Chambliss and Ben, and with Jess's mother wounded and most likely uninterested in returning home, Cash leaves us with an image of the onetime deserter of family redeeming his past by accepting his role as Jess's guardian. Adelaide Lyle concludes Jess's story by observing that Jimmy Hall brings the boy to church every Sunday, and notes that although the grandfather never enters the church himself, "It's enough for me to know that he's out there if Jess needs him. I think it's enough for Jess too" (306). Jess's story, then, although one of misfortune, ends on a hopeful note, a "rupture of optimism," as Locklear describes it ("Mountain Fatalism," 121). Both Jimmy and Jess move closer to redemption from their past actions through the healing embrace of family connections.

In Cash's second novel, *This Dark Road to Mercy* (2014), the setting shifts to Gastonia, North Carolina, in 1998, but the thematic focus continues the writer's reflections on the redemptive power of family relationships. Similarly, Cash maintains his concentration on child characters. The protagonist, twelve-year-old Easter Quillby, narrates her family's history as she tells of her and six-year-old sister Ruby's fatally drug-overdosed mother and their father, who is absent from their lives. Like Jess, Easter must grow up quickly, since, even before finding her mother dead, she essentially runs the household as an adult. After having abandoned the family several years earlier, the girls' father, Wade Chesterfield, a onetime minor-league baseball pitcher, gave up his rights to the children by signing a termination of parental rights form in 1996. Upon hearing of his former wife's death, Wade seeks to reconcile with his children, but Easter is skeptical, noting, "I'd always called him 'Wade' because it never felt right to think of him as 'Dad' or 'Daddy' or anything else that kids are supposed to call their parents" (2). As the plot progresses amid Wade's kidnapping of his children and his theft of a large sum of money and the subsequent travels through the Carolinas, Easter reveals her changing view of her father and the nature of his quest for family connection and redemption for his past destructive behavior.

Easter's willingness to accept her father's change solidifies when he defends the children at an ocean-side pavilion in Myrtle Beach, South Carolina. Having endured mockery and abuse from a group of wealthy teenagers earlier in the day, Easter encounters them again as the girls and their father toss baseballs at a pitching cage that measures the pitched balls' velocity. As Wade gives Easter fatherly advice on pitching, the teenagers interrupt this scene of genuine bonding between the father and his daughters by again mocking the girls' T-shirts. Wade approaches the four and good-naturedly asks if they play ball, eventually challenging the cockiest to a pitching contest. Wade's goal is to win a large teddy bear that the young man had previously won for his girlfriend. After a dramatic competition, Wade wins the bear for his daughters, but more significantly, he demonstrates his fatherly concern for his children's sense of self-worth. Noticing that her father has painfully achieved his goal, Easter recognizes the meaningful point of the gesture: "He'd thrown it because he knew those two boys were laughing at me, at us. It was the first time in my life that I felt like Wade wanted to be my dad" (99).

As the family struggles to stay ahead of law enforcement and a hired hit man charged with retrieving the stolen money and settling a personal grudge with Wade, they race through the Carolinas in disguise. Both Easter and Wade dye their hair brown, which matches Ruby's and the girls' mother's hair. As the three survey themselves in a mirror, Easter confides to the reader: "I felt like crying. The three of us finally looked like a family" (125). Eventually Wade divulges his goals to Easter: "I've only ever wanted two things in my whole life. The first was to play baseball, and I was good at it—real good—but I screwed up. . . . You and your sister are the second thing I want, something I never thought I'd have. . . . I just want a normal life, a normal house, a normal family" (135–36). Easter, having received her father's care over the course of a few days, reacts, again only to the reader: "I wanted to tell him that I'd always dreamed of having the exact same thing" (136). Easter's acceptance and Wade's redemption are not enough to keep the family together, however. Wade's illegal activities have made him the subject of a manhunt, and in a climactic scene, he must abandon his girls at a major-league baseball game.

But Cash does not stop telling the story there. He offers another hopeful narrative to complete the family's reconciliation. The girls are adopted by their maternal grandparents in Alaska, and they move there to live with their extended family. Like Jess and Jimmy Hall, Easter and Ruby find a home with family members they have never known. Easter reveals that she and Ruby are comfortable in their new home, where she hears strange voices telling them "how happy they were that me and Ruby had come to live with them" (228). But Wade has not disappeared from the picture. A package from a nearby town arrives with a typed letter welcoming the children to their new home. Inside the pocket of the stuffed teddy bear that the box contains, Easter finds a ticket stub to the game they attended with Wade, along with his final fatherly advice handwritten on the back: "Stay on base" (230). Cash stops telling the story here, with the children safely in a caring familial home, and Easter assured that her father indeed loves her.

The most structurally intricate of the novels, *The Last Ballad* (2017), presents these themes of redemption and family less overtly. Presented from the perspective of nine characters with complex family dynamics, the narrative moves through the turbulent labor struggles in Gaston County, North Carolina, from May through September 1929. Through flashbacks of characters' lives, Cash also builds the family histories of these characters, who range from textile workers to mill owners. Cash plucked the novel's protagonist, Ella May Wiggins, from the region's history of labor unrest and created a novel that focuses on labor, class, and racism. Although it is a less overt theme, the idea of family plays a large role in the plot, as Wiggins struggles to feed and clothe her own children while working to organize and integrate the union in Gaston County. Cash expands the concept of family here by emphasizing Wiggins's dedication to her community (she lives in a workers' camp primarily inhabited by Blacks) and the struggles of the nascent union, both of which serve as extended families. In this complex novel, Cash's masterful intertwining of fictional and historical characters' voices enables him to tell numerous stories of family and redemption, ranging from Wiggins's efforts to maintain her single-parent family, to the connections made between a Black textile worker and a northern Pullman porter, to the life-saving actions of a wealthy mill owner.

The mother of five children, four still alive, Ella seemingly neglects her family while pursuing the creation of a union in the Gaston County textile mills. Careful reading, however, reveals her devotion to her children, who range in age from eleven-year-old Lilly to one-year-old Wink. The novel begins with Ella being reprimanded by her employer for missing a shift because she was caring for her sick child, and later Cash underscores her motherly instinct by presenting an affectionate moment in the family's home: "Ella sat down beside Otis and picked up Wink, set him in her lap. She rubbed her nose against his head, felt the soft fuzz of his hair on her lips, looked down at his grasping baby hands. She touched Rose's face, felt the fatback grease on the little girl's lips, used her thumb to wipe it away" (35). Later in the novel, after Ella has left the children in the care of a neighbor while she attends a union rally, Cash demonstrates Ella's parental care as she reflects on her children: "Ella was starving and she pictured the cold stove and empty skillet back home in Stumptown, pictured her children relieved and smiling to be at Violet's mother's house, their bellies probably fuller than they'd been in days. Her heart swelled at the thought of their happiness" (109). We see Ella's devotion to her children, and yet she increasingly leaves her daughter Lilly in charge as the young mother becomes more involved in the union movement.

Ella's organizing efforts arise initially from her songwriting skills, and even the first lines of her most famous song, "The Mill Mother's Lament," emphasize the importance of caring for a family.

We leave our homes in the morning,
We kiss our children good-bye.

While we slave for the bosses,
Our children scream and cry.

Subsequent verses further note the deprivation of working for low wages, as mothers cannot afford both food and clothing. The answer, she writes in the final verse, lies in the formation of the union—one big family.

But understand, dear workers,
Our union they do fear.
Let's stand together, workers,
And have a union here. (106–7)

As the novel progresses, Cash emphasizes Ella's growing involvement in the union, and we see her spend less time with her children. Another voice, however, narrates the effect of her choices on her family. Lilly, eleven years old at the time of her mother's union activity and murder, offers a first-person account of her life and her mother's role in it. Presented as a letter to her nephew, eighty-seven-year-old Lilly's comments reveal her hard life but indicate that there was a blessing in it as well. She explains, "Everything about my mother has always amazed me" (54), even though others made her feel ashamed for being Ella's daughter. Lilly continues by recounting her memory of a visit by a Black man to the children's home where she had been sent after her mother's murder. The man, Hampton Haywood, is a Pullman porter who had been a northern organizer sent in 1929 to integrate the union in North Carolina. His story forms one part of the novel, but at this point, he plays a role in the redemption of Ella's actions. He delivers a letter from Sophia, another northern organizer, addressed to Lilly and her siblings, declaring Sophia's promise "to carry on her [Ella's] work of seeking justice and inspiring humanity and bringing together people of all races, for these are the reasons they killed her" (369). This sentiment touches Lilly, but Haywood's comments leave a more powerful impression. "Your mother saved my life. . . . She was a hero. Not just to me, but to a lot of people" (369), he tells Lilly, who notes to her nephew, "I didn't doubt him for a minute, though. I knew it was true. I know it's still true" (369–70).

Lilly's acceptance of her mother's role in many people's lives, not just those of her family, extends Cash's message from his earlier novels: despite one's actions, redemption can ultimately occur, most often within the family structure. In *The Last Ballad*, he demonstrates that while one's actions affect those nearest to him or her, a larger, lasting effect may also result. And in Cash's novels, this is a positive outcome. Writing about *A Land More Kind Than Home*, Locklear notes that the novel "features an ending that combines both tragedy and cautious optimism" ("Mountain Fatalism," 117). Similarly, the novelist Laird Hunt declares that *The Last Ballad* maintains "the sense of hope inherent in a movement that eventually brought change not just to North Carolina but to an entire nation" (3). Hope and optimism pervade Cash's novels, despite the often dark and violent events that surround his characters. His writing presents a perspective that suggests that such events, while scarring characters, may encourage growth and acceptance among those who survive. Lilly Wiggins's comment also says much about the importance of one's perspective on life: "Every story, even your own, is either happy or sad depending on where you stop telling it" (370). Wiley Cash's novels offer readers the opportunity to reflect on the beneficial results of negatively perceived actions and events in their own lives. Depending on how we see it, our lives can be happy or sad. In his novels, Cash opts for happy.

Works Cited

Cash, Wiley. *A Land More Kind Than Home*. HarperCollins, 2012.

Cash, Wiley. *The Last Ballad*. William Morrow, 2017.

Cash, Wiley. "Many Souths: An Interview with Wiley Cash." Interview with Brad Wetherell. *Fiction Writers Review*, April 17, 2012. https://fictionwritersreview.com/interview/many -souths-an-interview-with-wiley-cash. Accessed December 1, 2018.

Cash, Wiley. *This Dark Road to Mercy*. William Morrow, 2014.

Clark, Amy. "Wiley Cash." *Appalachian Heritage* 43, no. 2 (2015): 64–73.

Hovis, George. "The Legacy of Thomas Wolfe in Contemporary Appalachian Fiction: Four Recent North Carolina Novels." *Thomas Wolfe Review* 36, nos. 1–2 (2012): 70–91.

Hunt, Laird. "*The Last Ballad* by Wiley Cash Review: Murder in the Shadow of the Mills." *The Guardian*, January 10, 2018. https://www.theguardian.com/books/2018/jan/10/the-last -ballad-wiley-cash-review. Accessed December 1, 2018.

Locklear, Erica Abrams. "Mountain Fatalism in Wiley Cash's *A Land More Kind Than Home*." *Appalachian Heritage* 42, no. 3 (2014): 110–21.

David Armand, born and raised in Louisiana, has worked as a drywall hanger, a draftsman, and a press operator in a flag-printing factory. He is currently writer-in-residence at Southeastern Louisiana University, where he also serves as associate editor for Louisiana Literature Press. In 2010 he won the George Garrett Fiction Prize for his first novel, *The Pugilist's Wife*, published by Texas Review Press. His second novel, *Harlow*, was published by Texas Review Press in 2013. In 2015, David's third novel, *The Gorge*, was published by Southeast Missouri State University Press, and his poetry chapbook, *The Deep Woods*, by Blue Horse Press. David's memoir, *My Mother's House*, was published in 2016 by Texas Review Press. His latest poetry chapbook, *Debt*, was released in 2018 by Blue Horse Press. His seventh book, *The Lord's Acre*, appeared in 2020, and a second memoir is forthcoming.

"In Your Heart"

The Emotive Landscapes and Characters of David Armand's Rough South

Dixon Hearne

While David Armand's creative output has certainly been varied in terms of genre and mode of expression, one common feature in all his work links it inextricably to that of southern writers such as Flannery O'Connor, William Faulkner, and Cormac McCarthy: the use of southern settings to deal with distinctly American—and even universal—themes. Ultimately, all of Armand's work seems to be about one thing: the need for human connection. Furthermore, the theme arises in the context of what is often referred to as "Rough South" or "Grit Lit" fiction, as in the work of authors such as Larry Brown, Harry Crews, Tom Franklin, and others who have had similar backgrounds and experiences and have gone on to employ those experiences in their own creative work; but Armand tends to scoff at such labels. In an interview with Emily Choate, Armand stated:

> I don't particularly care for the term "Grit Lit," to be completely honest, as I feel like with any label, it sort of tries to pigeonhole works of art into a tidy little category. Sure, my work may be gritty in nature, but I think the term "Grit Lit" kind of serves as a short cut to real analysis, real thinking about the written work in terms of what it really is: and that is a story that tries to say something new (and *hopeful*) about the human condition.

In staking his claim as a southern writer aspiring to be an artist with universal appeal, Armand obviously alludes to William Faulkner's Nobel Prize acceptance speech. In that 1950 address, Faulkner said, "The problems of the human heart in conflict with itself . . . alone can make good writing because only that is worth writing about, worth the agony and the sweat." But that does not necessarily mean that Armand's work *shouldn't* be part of the canon of so-called Rough South writers, too, as his work clearly adheres to some of the tenets of the genre, and he has obviously been influenced by its practitioners.

Armand's work—much like that of Crews, Brown, Franklin, and Ron Rash—attempts to use *place* as a sort of character in and of itself, all to show the influence of a particular geography on the people who inhabit it, especially those of blue-collar, lower-middle-class backgrounds. Armand has written about the rural South and its people in his memoir, *My Mother's House*, and in a handful of nonfiction essays similar in style and scope to the writings of Harry Crews and Larry Brown, particularly in a piece from *Deep South Magazine* titled "Independence Day," in which Armand writes:

> Growing up in rural Louisiana meant three things during the summer: the days were long, hot, and—if you were poor, like I was—boring. It seemed as though there was never anything to do. The days melted into each other so that time became somewhat amorphous, one long gulp of it that stretched like taffy—all the way from May until school started back up again in August. It was kind of like that Salvador Dali painting, all those drooping clocks in the desert.
>
> To make things worse, my mother didn't have a car, and so we lived somewhat isolated in a singlewide trailer in the middle of a patch of cleared land, which was surrounded by thick pine woods.

The sense of *time* informs Armand's work as well—the simple abundance of it throughout his early life growing up in the country, and how that is likely responsible for his relaxed and conversational style of writing, whether in fiction, nonfiction, or poetry: short, staccato sentences followed by long, circuitous passages evoke the mysterious rivers and swaths of woods that blanket Armand's work. An excerpt from *The Gorge*, Armand's third novel, exemplifies the style:

> She watched the thin tendrils of flame whipping up at the sky and worrying the branches overhead with sparks: they moved under the visible

heat. The dry, brown leaves hanging from the trees along the embankment cracked and hissed.

The deepest ditch of night was falling upon them, and it seemed the hour was none. Their fire had died down to a smoldering pile of gray and orange ash. Some of the charred branches stuck out from the burnpile, and smoke leaked from their still-hot surfaces. Chantelle lay on her back in the sandy clay and looked up at the trees. Amber and Tuller lay across from her with their arms around each other. They were all smoking cigarettes and looking upward, but no one was saying anything. (18)

In scenes such as this, it is as though the landscape—in this case, the craggy escarpment of the gorge itself—shapes the prose and the stylistic choices the author makes, reminiscent of earlier practitioners of southern literature like Faulkner and McCarthy. This geography influences Armand's *characters* as well, forcing them to make difficult and what might otherwise seem like inexplicable choices, as in his first novel, *The Pugilist's Wife*:

Joe Wallace has been walking for two days now through these thick unforgiving woods, the tall narrow trees jutting out from the ground like crooked black fingers. The dead branches on the ground get caught around his ankles and feet as he walks. Yet he persists, slicing his way through the woods like a shiv. He doesnt know how exactly he ended up here, how it is that he is wandering with no food or drink, no real idea of where he is going now. But he knows this: he is in these woods, and he has to end up somewhere or he will die. And he does not want to die. He knows this too, feels it. It's in his gut. (5)

Here the reader can see a character not only interacting with the landscape but also being *consumed* by it, forced to decide between life and death. In this novel, the reader sees that Joe Wallace is ultimately looking for human connection, relief from the oppressive, threatening setting.

Armand's work, then, uses southern settings to deal with the American, even universal, theme of searching for human connection; at the same time, it adheres to the school of Rough South writers in its depiction of a hardscrabble environment and its denizens. His second novel, *Harlow*, which tells the archetypal story of a boy searching for his father, provides a clear example of this combination, opening with a long paragraph reminiscent of the opening of Cormac McCarthy's *Blood Meridian*:

It was dark. The boy lay down in a swale and rolled the flannel shirt he had been wearing into a cigarette shaped pillow and placed it under his head. He closed his eyes and tried to sleep as the crickets played a steady hum in the woods around him. A car occasionally drove over the gravelroad beyond him, throwing rocks and dirt down and over near the ditchbank where the boy lay shivering now, the red clay loosening from the embankment and powdering the boy's clothes and skin a strange ocher. He tucked his knees into his chest and rubbed his cheek against the warm flannel and looked peripherally at the clear winter sky overhead. Each white star and the full white moon seemed holes punched into the myriad blackness surrounding everything: the only thing darker—more black—the pine trees jutting from the ground like crooked black teeth against the cold and hollow mouth of sky behind them. (5)

Here again the reader sees a character not only influenced by the rough landscape surrounding him, but a boy who, like Joe Wallace in *The Pugilist's Wife*, is almost literally being *swallowed up* by that landscape. The only way to escape, it would seem, is to find some sort of human connection, which *Harlow*'s young protagonist, Leslie, is trying to do by searching for his father. Armand employs similar physical descriptions in all three of his novels. He further links them by presenting characters who share the same motives and desires: to connect with others on an emotional level. Again like Faulkner, Armand is attempting to create a *world* with his entire corpus of work, one in which characters meander from book to book, much like the Snopeses in Faulkner's Yoknapatawpha County.

Harlow works to do all these things, and more, in a style that Doug Childers, in the *Richmond Times-Dispatch*, called "a comfortably familiar literary voice that blends Ernest Hemingway's laconic but rhythmically complicated explorations of the mysteries of masculinity with William Faulkner's more fabulist, Southern Gothic twang." The publication later named the novel a Top-Five Fiction Book of the Year for 2013, alongside works by George Saunders, John Ralston Saul, Stephen King, and Nobel laureate J. M. Coetzee. This recognition demonstrates that Armand's realistic and "rough" southern settings have the ability to evoke universal themes for a broad readership. Further, a review published in the *Southern Literary Review* notes:

Armand's Leslie Somers . . . finds himself cast off into the adult world with but his wits and a burning search for some sense of legitimacy [and] is

acutely haunted by a deep sense of incompleteness. . . . *Harlow* also features
encounters with an odd array of "freakish" people and events: an armless
man at a parish fair who throws darts with his toes; a young woman with a
deformed spine; a Christian zealot who robs because Christ compels him to
do so. (Hearne, "*Harlow*")

These words encapsulate not only Armand's interest in universality but also
his sympathetic portrayal of "Rough South" or "Grit Lit" characters, often
referred to as "grotesque," but once explained well by Flannery O'Connor:
"When you can assume that your audience holds the same beliefs you do,
you can relax and use more normal means of talking to it; when you have
to assume that it does not, then you have to make your vision apparent by
shock—to the hard of hearing you shout, and for the almost-blind you draw
large and startling figures" (34). This strategy can be perilous when artists
fall into the trap of caricature or stereotype in such portrayals; however,
Armand's background—similar to that of Harry Crews, Larry Brown, and
Tom Franklin, who also all grew up poor and in the South—seems to have
a great impact on his realistic and empathetic depictions of the people who
inhabit his fiction. He is a writer who seems to have taken to heart the old
adage "write what you know."

Armand's work, then, relies heavily on a strong sense of place, which
at once anchors it to a sort of southern literary tradition of storytelling
while also enabling him to provide a stage, like Shakespeare's, on which his
characters may enact their own *universal* dramas. As Armand has stated in
an interview with *Fiction Writers Review*:

When I first started writing in earnest, I thought that I had to write about
places that everyone knew about—you know, the big cities, the places we see
in movies. My teacher, Tim Gautreaux, told me that I had better look around
where I was and write about that. Not only would it be more authentic, he
said, but I would have an easier time of it since I knew this place so well. He
was absolutely right, too. Once I started setting my fiction here in Louisiana
in the small towns with which I was familiar, my stories started to take on an
authenticity they didn't have before. Now I feel as though this place, the "toe"
on the boot that is southeastern Louisiana, is my "little postage stamp" and
that I would be doing a great disservice to my fiction, to my readers, and to
myself if I ever wrote about any other place. ("Native Soil")

This is nothing new, of course. Writers from the South typically write with a strong sense of place. Armand creates a paradox in his work: a place can be at once menacing and brutal yet simultaneously essential for survival. It is a world, according to Stephen Febick, that Armand paints "with simplicity and darkness, carrying us through wide-open fields, houses that have been abandoned, dirt roads, and mystery." But for the artist who is documenting this "rough South," perhaps the reasons for doing so are less about mystery and more in line with what Margaret Renkl has said in a *New York Times* piece in 2018: "Maybe being a Southern writer is only a matter of loving a damaged and damaging place, of loving its flawed and beautiful people, so much that you have to stay there, observing and recording and believing, against all odds, that one day it will finally live up to the promise of its own good heart."

And it is "heart" that seems to be at the center of Armand's work. Whether through fiction, nonfiction, or poetry, it is the heart of a place—southeastern Louisiana—and the heart of the characters about whom he writes that elevates all his work. His southern setting speaks to universal themes. The closing line of his novel *Harlow* even reads, "So keep it there where it is written: in your heart" (166), the biblical allusion making it clear that Armand's concerns extend beyond just southern storytelling.

Even Armand's memoir, *My Mother's House*, elicits a universal point about mental illness, through a highly specific lens. The memoir tackles the issue of mental illness and the way it is treated (or mistreated) in Louisiana, ultimately becoming a critique of the *entire country's* flaws in dealing with the mentally ill. In keeping with the tradition of Rough South writing, Armand relays in candid detail the story of his childhood: being born to a schizophrenic mother, only to be adopted and raised by an alcoholic stepfather. This seemingly hardscrabble childhood—similar to that described in Crews's *A Childhood: The Biography of a Place*—without a doubt informs Armand's Rough South aesthetic throughout his entire body of work, in which he writes in great detail about violence, alcoholism, drug abuse, and the "damaged and damaging place" in which he grew up.

But Armand's work never loses its sense of hope. As evidenced in his body of writing, he seems to believe what Faulkner said in that Nobel speech, that "man will not merely endure: he will prevail. He is immortal, not because he alone among creatures has an inexhaustible voice, but because he has a soul, a spirit capable of compassion and sacrifice and endurance." The closing lines of *My Mother's House* seem to echo this sentiment: "I hope that one day something can be done to better help people like my mother. I hope that all of the mentally ill, the downtrodden, the addicted, the hopeless, the forlorn, all of them can get the care that they need, that they deserve. And I hope that one day perhaps I can help make that happen. Maybe this is a start" (185).

Ultimately, despite his distaste for the labels "Rough South" and "Grit Lit," Armand's work clearly continues in that tradition, further using *place* as a somewhat dichotomous (both "damaged and damaging") character in his narratives to highlight the downtrodden and desperate people who inhabit it, ultimately tackling distinctively American—even universal—themes. And much in the same vein as his Rough South predecessors Crews, Brown, O'Connor, and McCarthy, Armand uses violence and often "large and startling figures" to make his point that while his is not an easy place to live in, that tiny speck of hope always dances in the distance, shimmering and never completely out of reach. And like all literature that aspires to transcend its genre and its place, Armand uses this distinct southern setting, his "own little postage stamp of native soil" of southeast Louisiana, to wrestle with the universal theme of one's constant and hopeful search for human connection. The closing line of Armand's poem "Mischief" expresses the idea succinctly: "until someone stops them, says, 'Come here, son. I love you.'" That hope, or something quite like it, sustains us all.

Works Cited

Armand, David. *The Gorge*. Southeast Missouri State University Press, 2015.

Armand, David. *Harlow*. Texas Review Press, 2013.

Armand, David. "Independence Day." *Deep South Magazine*, July 3, 2018. https://www.deep southmag.com/2018/07/03/independence-day. Accessed November 16, 2018.

Armand, David. "Mischief." In *Debt*, by David Armand, 32–33. Blue Horse Press, 2018.

Armand, David. *My Mother's House*. Texas Review Press, 2016.

Armand, David. "Native Soil: An Interview with David Armand." Interview with Dixon Hearne. *Fiction Writers Review*, October 17, 2014. https://www.fictionwritersreview.com /interview/native-soil-an-interview-with-david-armand. Accessed November 16, 2018.

Armand, David. *The Pugilist's Wife*. Texas Review Press, 2011.

Childers, Doug. "Doug Childers's Favorite Books of 2013." *Richmond Times-Dispatch*, December 15, 2013. https://www.richmond.com/entertainment/books/books-doug-childers -favorite-books-of/article_4ed3196b-da34-58e2-b284-9c612f0ddaa0.html. Accessed November 16, 2018.

Choate, Emily. "David Armand: *The Gorge*." *Late Night Library*, October 5, 2015. https://www .latenightlibrary.org/david-armand. Accessed November 16, 2018.

Faulkner, William. "Banquet Speech." The Nobel Prize. https://www.nobelprize.org/prizes
/literature/1949/faulkner/speech. Accessed September 3, 2018.

Febick, Stephen. "*The Gorge* by David Armand." *Portland Book Review*, April 15, 2016. https://
www.portlandbookreview.com/2016/04/the-gorge-by-david-armand. Accessed November
16, 2018.

Hearne, Dixon. "*Harlow*, by David Armand." *Southern Literary Review*, May 7, 2014. https://www
.southernlitreview.com/reviews/may-read-of-the-month-harlow-by-david-armand.html.
Accessed September 3, 2018.

O'Connor, Flannery. "The Fiction Writer and His Country." In *Mystery and Manners:
Occasional Prose*, by Flannery O'Connor. Farrar, Straus and Giroux, 1969, 25–35.

Renkl, Margaret. "What Is a Southern Writer, Anyway?" *New York Times*, July 9, 2018. https://
www.nytimes.com/2018/07/09/opinion/what-is-a-southern-writer.html. Accessed
November 16, 2018.

Karen Russell (b. July 10, 1981) was born in Miami, Florida. She earned a BA from Northwestern University and an MFA from Columbia University. Known for her work at the border of fantasy and psychological realism, she has published several collections of short fiction and two novels. Her debut novel, *Swamplandia!*, was a finalist for the 2012 Pulitzer Prize for Fiction; in 2013 she received a MacArthur Fellowship. She has been a Guggenheim Fellow (2011) and a fellow at the American Academy of Berlin (2012) and has taught writing and literature at numerous colleges and universities throughout the United States.

Karen Russell

A South without Borders

Melanie Benson Taylor

Here is an island where the raised bogs are threatened by industrial harvesters, where nobody quite remembers the old stories, and the remaining islanders have only a staticky sense of
their ancient language and history. But the landscape itself still
retains this oneiric power, and a humming autonomy—that's the
sublimity of places like swamps and bogs, I think, and also of
mountains and ocean trenches, landscapes that resize you, landscapes that are uncanny reminders of the brevity of a human
lifespan and the vastness of geologic time.
—KAREN RUSSELL, interview with Willing Davidson (2016)

Karen Russell's world is almost indescribably vast. She is an American
writer, but her United States is a space in a perpetual state of discovery,
her characters always facing a frontier of some ponderous sort. While she
is first and foremost a southern writer, she writes about a region we have
never seen in quite this way before: the Florida Everglades poised perpetually
on the brink of encounter and apocalypse all at once, peopled by lost and
searching tribes that exist just out of view of mainstream culture. Throughout,
her fiction haunts the fluid borders between life and death, history and the
present, fantasy and reality, island and mainland, human and animal. Her

protagonists are often young people navigating uncharted terrain or spectral encounters, usually without adult supervision—a viewpoint that contributes to her stories' uncanny wonder. But while these narrative perspectives are disarmingly smart and frequently comic, the settings and journeys they survey are the real subject of the fiction: "oneiric" spaces with deep histories and "autonomy," bequeathing lessons as old and as vast as the earth itself—"landscapes that resize you," as Russell puts it.

Russell's three short story collections, *St. Lucy's Home for Girls Raised by Wolves* (2007), *Vampires in the Lemon Grove* (2014), and *Orange World and Other Stories* (2019), offer numerous, eclectic variations on this theme. The stories themselves are inestimably diverse and their settings far-flung: a workers' revolt by half-women, half-silkworm laborers in a Japanese factory in 1844 ("Reeling for the Empire"); a vampire couple in Italy who attempt, but fail miserably, to convert their diet from blood to lemons ("Vampires in the Lemon Grove"); two young brothers search for their dead sister, who floated away on a crab shell ("Haunting Olivia"); a massage therapist can alter a veteran's memories by rearranging the details of his tattoo ("The New Veterans"); two settler families in Homestead-era Nebraska share a glass window (a requirement for landownership), only to have it taken back by the ghost of a former settler ("Proving Up"); another pioneer family travels west—but the dad is a minotaur ("Children's Reminiscences of the Western Migration").

The premises of these stories are nothing if not odd. But the narratives themselves revolve around disarmingly human, accessible interior crises and reflections. Russell's characters seem to wonder in a stunning variety of ways, *what does it mean to be human?* The answers are elusive: they involve searches for memory and truth across vast landscapes of time, geography, and cultures, and more often than not, they testify to the failures of such quests under the tyranny of a suffocating present. Yet her characters remain haunted by their desires and stubbornly refuse to admit defeat. Often they inhabit island or coastal communities where oceans and swamps guard mysteries that tantalize. In "The Prospectors," two teenage girls travel from East Coast to West, away from a Depression-era tourist community in Florida where "a sea serpent, it was rumored, haunted the coastline beside the hotel, and ninety per cent of our tourism was serpent-driven." They arrive at a new resort on an Oregon mountain that seems a clear echo of *The Shining*'s Overlook Hotel, which indeed was modeled on Mount Hood's Timberline Lodge, the same building that inspired Russell. Like Stanley Kubrick's hotel, this one too is haunted—by the ghosts of the workers who attempted to build it. The girls refer to themselves as "prospectors," as they are hunting for both material and intangible rewards out West, yet they realize in the end that the seductive frontier is a dangerous fantasy. They are scarcely more alive than the ghosts they flirt with, and the vast Pacific landscape might as well be home: the first-person narrator recalls a man who "whispered to [her] once, too sozzled to remember [her] name, 'Thank you . . . for keeping the secret that there is no secret.' The black Atlantic rippled emptily in his eyeglasses." The emptiness of the outer rims of these worlds shadows and threatens, even as the characters resist them; whatever knowledge they harbor is inscrutable, possibly insupportable. In "The Bog Girl," a story set on an island of Ireland, a teenage boy finds—and dates—a woman who has been preserved in a swamp for thousands of years; in the end, she comes alive, and he rejects her, no longer the blank, submissive template for his desires and fantasies.

This illicit romance with the dead is a trope that recurs in various ways throughout Russell's fiction. More often than not, the ghosts seduce the living because they are freighted with destructive knowledge: that of the imperial histories that have settled in their bodies and, in many cases, precipitated their ruin. In "The Prospectors," the narrator realizes with a shock that all the very lively men they meet are in fact "dead—ensconced in a coffin of their own making, the structure they built, with gold arrested in their eyes." The building itself, dazzled with its own irruptive beauty, "wanted to go on shining in our living eyes." Indeed, the explored, built world and the natural one alike converge on human substance: going west is always a trope for self-discovery in Russell's fiction, and bodies themselves become uncanny maps. An abused girl's bruises are "mute blue coordinates" ("Prospectors"); the swamp's "fetally scrolled bodies often [double] as the crumpled maps of murders" ("The Bog Girl"). Neither entity exists without the other, and yet they live in uneasy counterpoise, both demanding and refusing admittance and true intimacy. Russell's characters are always yearning to connect more deeply but failing to do so, adrift at the edges of histories that have literally blown them apart.

Swamplandia! is Russell's debut novel and her most complete expression of her preferred themes and methods. It was short-listed for the Pulitzer Prize in 2012. The narrative centers on an eponymous alligator-wrestling theme park run by the Bigtree family in the Florida Everglades. As the novel opens, the business is in shambles after the death of the mother, Hilola, to cancer; the remaining family members—the father, whom the kids call "Chief," and teenagers Kiwi, Osceola (nicknamed "Ossie"), and the narrator and protagonist, Ava—struggle to recuperate both family and livelihood after the loss of Swamplandia!'s star and matriarch. Chief takes regular trips to the mainland to earn money; Kiwi leaves to work at a competitor's theme park, the World of Darkness; Ossie wanders the swamps at night, "dating" ghosts; and Ava, the youngest at thirteen, is left behind, trying to keep the place together and to nurse a strange red alligator hatchling that she has secreted away. The story's climax comes when Ossie elopes with the ghost of a WPA-era dredgeman named Louis Thanksgiving, and Ava goes on a journey to rescue Ossie from what she believes to be the underworld, guided by a strange Bird Man who shows up on the family property one day.

It is no secret to anyone—neither readers nor the characters themselves—that the Bigtrees are playing Indian unreflectively and unapologetically. "Although there was not a drop of Seminole or Miccosukee in us," Ava reports, "the Chief always costumed us in tribal apparel for the photographs he took. He said we were 'our own Indians'" (6). He even rewrites the family history at will, lodging the records in the on-site Bigtree Museum: "Certain artifacts appeared or vanished, dates changed and old events appeared in fresh blue ink on new cards beneath the dusty exhibits. . . . You had to pretend like the Bigtree story had always read that way" (32). The Bigtrees are, in fact, the white descendants of a coal miner from Ohio, Ernest Shedrach, who chooses the name "Sawtooth" in honor of the island's sedge, and "Bigtree" appealed to him with its "root-strong," indigenous sound (31); in one swift act of self-reclamation, he and his descendants are reborn as Natives. On a tiny, swampy island in the Everglades reachable only by ferry, the Shedrachs-cum-Bigtrees effectively function as proxies for America's second-wave settlement of weary pioneers, looking to flee the hardscrabble industrialism of the early twentieth century in the wild, purchasing a "hundred-acre waste" marketed rhapsodically by northern realtors as the "American Eden" (31). There they launch a gator-wrestling dynasty—a vocation with an illustrious indigenous pedigree, particularly among local Seminoles.

The Everglades, close to Russell's own native Miami, prove an unconventional setting for Russell's indigenous/pioneer story; but for Russell, it is just the right space, a swampy pocket of national history that might otherwise be forgotten by mainstream culture. For the area's inhabitants, though, those histories persist in uncanny, often bodily ways. The Everglades have often been deemed America's last frontier, wild and untouched well after the closing of the western frontier. As Michael Grunwald describes in *The Swamp*, the vast wetland is an unambiguous national treasure, capable of inspiring broad bipartisan support for measures to preserve and restore it; it is, he claims, "the ecological equivalent of motherhood and apple pie," and he recalls an episode of NBC's *The West Wing* in which an aide said that the most popular thing the president could do for the environment would be to "save the Everglades" (4). Of course, this was not always the case: in the early days of its discovery, the swamp was deemed a "useless bog" that needed to be drained and developed. Today, Grunwald reports, the Everglades are a "tattered battlefield": half is "gone"; the other half "is an ecological mess" (3–6). For Russell, this would be a space to wonder at and explore in her fiction, which she often transferred onto other such swampy, haunted sites, not just in America but globally.

Indeed, while her characters are idiosyncratic and their crises acutely private, Russell's themes are always expansive, nearly panoramic in their scope. Here Russell dramatizes the cataclysm of America's mythologies about settlement and industrial development with the story of Louis Thanksgiving, a member of the WPA dredge crew that ends up executing the opposite of "conservation" in their efforts to dredge and tame the swamp. Louis's European ancestry, like the Shedrach name, had already been cast aside by the miracle of his birth: he was "born dead" to an immigrant mother who died during childbirth, yet he revived miraculously and was thus christened "Thanksgiving." In his name is encoded the fictional harmony of the European settler and the indigenous host, the narrative of rebirth and the particularly American delusion of consecrated beginnings. Louis does not survive in the way that Sawtooth does; a terrible accident kills Louis and several of his mates, effectively slaying their "fraternity" of the American working class (138). His death, in fact, seems the point of his story: he embodies the perilous illusion of a life sustained by fantasy and foolhardiness and the haunting limits of America's exploratory and multicultural fantasies.

Russell once told an interviewer:

This book grew out of my sense that I had arrived a little late for the party, that a few generations ago . . . the Everglades was a wonderland. I grew up in a time when there was an increased consciousness of phosphor solution and development . . . [a] reckoning with the past twenty years of development and its consequences. So I think it must always be the case that you are in the shadow of an Eden that was more spectacular than your own. ("Karen Russell on *Swamplandia!*")

Russell's characters hunger to retrieve that paradise, even as they learn increasingly that its very existence is an illusion—a rippling emptiness. The appeal of indigeneity surfaces repeatedly as an antidote, but Russell and her characters know, at some suppressed level (and often too late), that the guise is a ruse. The most pernicious container for this lesson is the mysterious Bird Man who befriends and then betrays and rapes Ava. He sports a boat built on an old Seminole blueprint and spouts swamp wisdom gleaned from gator hunters, moonshiners, and Indians alike: "Nobody can get to hell without assistance, kid" (183). The most wounding revelation of all is that this fake Indian rapist seems to be right: that is, the fatal logic in this book suggests that human companions might be our salvation when, in fact, they are frequently our ruin. Literally, Ava thinks the Bird Man is assisting her in getting to hell—or to the fabled entrance to the underworld, which is, importantly, marked by a pair of ancient Calusa Indian mounds. The Bird Man navigates this indigenous terrain with apparent ease: he is not an Indian per se, but he lives and dresses simply like one, and with his makeshift Seminole craft and navigational system, he leads her directly into the portals of fantasy. Predictably, their mission soon implodes: the "underworld" is emphatically alive, Ossie is nowhere to be found, and the Bird Man takes advantage of Ava's desire for intimacy by sexually assaulting her. Ava eventually manages to escape from the Bird Man, and in her harrowing journey back home, her entire body is "dyed a black-maroon from the tannins" in the swamp—"at last I'd turned the color of a real Indian," she marvels (342). The natural world imbues her once again with, at the least, the "color" and spirit of resistance against the world's cruelest deceptions, and we do not miss the irony that Indigenous pageantry—whether the Bigtrees' or the Bird Man's—is a route to nowhere. As Christopher Rieger points out, the Bird Man's character draws on a composite cache of indigenous folklore, only to underscore in the end the pernicious distortions of Native culture demonstrated throughout the novel.

Russell's fiction thus offers magic that seems painfully double-fisted: it offers a knowledge and salvation that her characters believe in desperately and ingenuously, even if it wounds them—as it always does. Indeed, part of the coming-of-age process in the novel seems to be reckoning with the terrible,

mundane realities behind the fecund landscape of dreams that functions
edenically for Americans worn down by industrial development, debt, and
depression. In this way, the novel invites history and fantasy together to blaze an
illuminating path into the Bigtrees' befuddled present. When the "lone Indian"
on Louis's WPA crew, Euphon Tigertail, is beaten by the Everglades' severe
environment and decides to leave, he urges Louis to escape with him: "You'll
go in there and never come out," he warns. But Louis stays on, with no past or
people to reclaim him, thinking, "How could you make a mistake when you had
one option?" (138). Russell underscores here the poverty of choice that fuels the
American dream, leaving seemingly one path to survival. As an allegory, Louis's
story suggests that Euphon Tigertail was right all along: the Indian instinct for
preservation is one's lifeline through the American wasteland of "progress"—a
place where you go in and "never come out." The catch, however, is that there
is nowhere else to go. Indeed, what depletes the Bigtree family most is not the
demise of the island ecosystem, but that of their tourist enterprise—which,
in their grave folly, they see as one and the same. Like the ghosts who refuse
to abandon the lodge in "The Prospectors," the Bigtree family deteriorates
along with the gator-wrestling enterprise they have overidentified with it: Ava
watches Kiwi's body deteriorate, "robbed of actual matter" (67), and sees herself
"evaporating" too (167). Kiwi defines the phenomenon as "convection": "the
rapid cooling of a body in the absence of all tourists" (236). Significantly, Kiwi
plumps up once on the mainland, eating fast food and accumulating "girlish
hips" (275). Ossie's response, too, is to consume—in large quantities, senselessly
and irrepressibly—grains of rice, sticks of butter, heads of cauliflower, frozen
steaks, and "Pick Up Club" meals: foods packaged, processed, and shipped
from the mainland. (It is presumably no accident either that her love interest
bears the name of the American holiday associated with gorging oneself
silly in a ceremony of patriotism and plenty.) Together, the Bigtree children
demonstrate physically the fateful progress of consumer capitalism and the
(literally) haunting reminder of our American romance with the feast. Without
the energy and profits of their business enterprise, they shift modes to pure
and voracious consumerism, their bodies hungry for more and more "Burger
Burger" and "Pick Up Club" satiation.

Like so many American and southern authors, Russell makes her
characters dance between these poles of faith and despair. In the end, Russell
seems no less immune than her characters to the power of the "dream," the
miracle, the antidote to being consumed whole by a world of darkness and

hunger and rape, even if the fable leaves us "bloated and rippling" or, like Ossie, drugged and docile and "paralytic" in the end (395). In the end, the Bigtree family begins a new life on the mainland, but Ava knows that they will never quite be free. In a closing line that could aptly summarize Russell's own artistic convictions—to compulsively demonstrate and perform history's disasters and seductions—Ava recalls "this cardboard clock [we used to have on Swamplandia!] and you could move the tiny hands to whatever time you wanted, NEXT SHOW AT __:__ O'CLOCK!" (397).

Works Cited

Grunwald, Michael. *The Swamp: The Everglades, Florida and the Politics of Paradise*. Simon & Schuster, 2007.

Rieger, Christopher. "From Childhood to the Underworld: Native American Birdman Iconography and Karen Russell's *Swamplandia!*" *Mississippi Quarterly* 68, no. 3 (Summer 2015): 399–414.

Russell, Karen. "The Bog Girl." *New Yorker*, June 20, 2016. https://www.newyorker.com/magazine /2016/06/20/bog-girl-by-karen-russell. Accessed October 30, 2018.

Russell, Karen. "Karen Russell on *Swamplandia!*" Interview with Nicole Rudick. *Paris Review*, February 3, 2011. https://www.theparisreview.org/blog/2011/02/03/karen-russell-on-swamp landia. Accessed October 30, 2018.

Russell, Karen. "The Prospectors." *New Yorker*, June 8–15, 2015. https://www.newyorker.com /magazine/2015/06/08/the-prospectors. Accessed September 18, 2018.

Russell, Karen. St. *Lucy's Home for Girls Raised by Wolves*. Vintage, 2007.

Russell, Karen. *Swamplandia!* Knopf, 2011.

Russell, Karen. *Vampires in the Lemon Grove and Other Stories*. Vintage, 2013.

Steph Post is the author of the novels *Walk in the Fire*, *Lightwood*, *A Tree Born Crooked*, *Miraculum*, and *Holding Smoke*. She graduated from Davidson College as a recipient of the Patricia Cornwell Scholarship for creative writing and a winner of the Vereen Bell Memorial Award for fiction. She holds a master's degree in graduate liberal studies from the University of North Carolina Wilmington. Her work has most recently appeared in *Garden & Gun*, *Nonbinary Review*, *CrimeReads*, and the anthology *Stephen King's Contemporary Classics*. She is a regular contributor to *Alternating Current* and *LitReactor* and has published numerous book reviews and author interviews. She has been nominated for a Pushcart Prize and a Rhysling Award and was a semifinalist for the Big Moose Prize. She lives in Florida.

Beauty in Brokenness
Steph Post's Rough South Noir

Amanda Dean Freeman

Steph Post's work falls in many ways squarely within the Rough South tradition, but it adds an element of noir and a cinematic flair that makes it easy to imagine her work being turned into a film or miniseries. Her casts of characters walk the line between working-class and criminal and find themselves on the wrong side of the law more often than not. Duffel bags full of cash change hands, friends and family betray each other, rival gangs find themselves face-to-face, and bullets always end up flying either through the neon-tinted light of a local bar or through the heavy, humid air of rural Florida—but these classic crime fiction tropes only serve to highlight more important themes that resonate through all of Post's work. The real heart of Post's fiction is her empathetic, fully fleshed-out treatment of lower-class, often criminal characters.

Post readily acknowledges her interest in championing those looked down on by society: "One of my goals as a writer is to tell stories about the underdogs, the losers, the people who only get stereotyped or used as foils, and to tell them beautifully. To give these characters as much dignity and respect as you would any character in the literary world" ("A Conversation"). Their relationships, their pain, their moral dilemmas, their dreams that have so little hope of ever being realized, create a warm pulse that beats beneath plotlines that might otherwise sound clichéd, forcing readers to see these people for who they are: human beings like everyone else.

Like many of her Rough South predecessors and contemporaries, Post did not initially plan on writing in either the so-called Grit Lit genre or the noir mode. She explains that she began simply by writing about what she knew best based on her upbringing in rural north-central Florida—an area of the state that beach-bound tourists rarely frequent. Given Post's rural southern settings and her passion for portraying down-and-out characters routinely marginalized by society, Rough South literature proved a natural fit. She was initially surprised when her agent marketed her work in the crime fiction world, but she came to realize that this genre too made sense: "The crime genre," Post says, "is probably the most welcoming and inclusive when it comes to the types of characters I like to read and write about. Crime fiction doesn't shy away from misfits, from complicated plots or from characters (and authors) living on the edge. The genre wasn't one that I expected to ever be a part of, but I've found that it's the perfect niche for me" ("'Lightwood' Author Steph Post"). This description could very well be applied to Rough South literature, and Post's work does in fact demonstrate remarkable thematic similarities with the Rough South and noir.

The protagonists that populate her fiction often feel trapped by their environment, by their poverty, and by their own families, but Post avoids formulaic victim narratives by demonstrating the complexity of these circumstances. Are the residents of these small, rural towns truly trapped, or do they inevitably return to their hometown because they love it despite themselves? Are their lives steered by fate or by choice? Even if they leave, will they ever truly be free from the family they left behind? Do they want to be? James Hart, the protagonist of *A Tree Born Crooked*, wrestles with these questions as he contemplates leaving his family and hometown forever after his father's death. Instead James finds himself helping his little brother Rabbit escape the culmination of his life of petty crime: a botched robbery, murder, and betrayal by his own cousin force Rabbit to go on the run. Racked with guilt at the thought of abandoning Rabbit, James reluctantly accompanies his brother, and his new friend Marlena accompanies them for similar reasons— her father helped orchestrate the failed burglary, and unless she and James can think of a plan to save Rabbit and Waylon, they will all die at the hands of the Alligator Mafia. The ensuing road trip to find Waylon and the missing money is rife with tension. All three suffer from an acute sense of loneliness and deep-seated resentment of family members who have betrayed them at one time or another, and James battles this inner vacuum by shutting out everyone around him.

Despite James's reticence, forging real human relationships proves to be the only bulwark against the pain of existence. James and Marlena's mutual suffering creates a sort of magnetism between them, and the rare quiet hours that occur over the next few days crystallize into moments of intimate, almost spiritual connection. James tells Marlena about a recurring dream in which he is a lone oak tree in a field in the dead of winter, and lightning strikes: "I can hear it, but I can't feel it. I've been struck by lightning and I'm splitting right down the middle. . . . But I don't catch on fire, and I don't die. I'm just broken. And I know that I'm gonna keep on growing, but only crooked" (140). Marlena responds, "We can't escape who we are, be that twisted or crooked or broken or even struck by lightning. . . . The important thing is just what you said, that you keep on growing. You keep living, and you keep breathing, even when it feels like your lungs are going to collapse and your heart is only an empty shell, you still keep on breathing" (141–42). James feels as if he is alone, but he is not the only tree born crooked in this book or in Post's ensuing novels.

All humans may be born crooked in some sense, but the people of these stories are not just born crooked; they are hit by lightning, battered repeatedly by storms, and simply can't catch a break even when they try their hardest to make all the right decisions. They have to put everything on the line almost daily just to survive, and the only thing that makes every difficult day worth it is the knowledge that they are not alone. In *Lightwood* and its sequel, *Walk in the Fire*, Post elaborates on this theme and shows beauty in brokenness. *A Tree Born Crooked* almost serves as a rehearsal for *Lightwood*; the two main characters resemble James and Marlena, but Post thickens the plot, accelerates the pace, and takes more time to create recognizable and memorable characters. She does not smooth over the rough edges of the people she creates, but she also refuses to infantilize or glorify them, and the result is a fast-paced thriller whose strength lies in the authenticity and rawness of its characters.

Lightwood commences with Judah Cannon emerging from prison utterly alone; no one greets him outside the gate, and he eventually makes his solitary way home to the town of Silas because he has nowhere else to go: "He knew that he was lost, though he would never have admitted it, and he knew that

Silas was not the swallow that was going to lead him to shore. If anything, the town would drown him, twisting its tentacles around his heart and dragging him down to the depths" (11–12). Judah's premonition proves truer than he could ever imagine. His ruthless father, Sherwood Cannon, runs a small-time criminal empire out of Silas, and in no time Judah is back in the clutches of the lawless Cannon ways that landed him behind bars in the first place. Based on an insider tip, the Cannons ambush a biker gang transporting a large load of cash—but they don't realize that half the money belongs to a malicious and merciless Pentecostal preacher, Sister Tulah. She will stop at nothing to retrieve what they stole, and Judah finds himself caught between his own clan, the Scorpion gang, and Sister Tulah.

Judah's poverty at first renders him practically powerless to break free from a lifelong cycle of criminality and violence. His own father lays Judah's situation out plainly in an effort to persuade his son to rejoin the family operation: "No job, no money, no skills, no way to make a future. In short, you got nothing. Without family, you got nothing. But with family, you got everything" (35). Judah feels himself being "backed into a familiar corner" (36), moving through his life as a supposedly free man like "a piece of Sargassum tossed about by the waves or warmed by the sun, but always at the direction of an element outside of himself" (118).

Post's female characters often demonstrate more self-awareness and agency. Ramey Barrow, Judah's closest childhood friend and now soul mate, is the only person who can save Judah from drowning. Ramey is tough, determined, courageous, and fiercely loyal, often prompting reviewers and interviewers to comment on Post's "badass" female characters (Catalano). Their shared suffering and long history connect Ramey and Judah, along with a sense that they are simply fated to be together. The bond between them seems stronger than blood, and Ramey's devotion to Judah appears ironclad; but fire, family, and fate will test their love time and time again, and Ramey has to compete with the Cannons both to preserve Judah's loyalty and to maintain his moral compass.

Despite the undeniably difficult situations many of the characters find themselves in, however, Post does not present their predicaments as hopeless or their decisions as meaningless. On the contrary, every decision made even by secondary characters bears great weight. As the novel's title suggests, each choice unwittingly becomes "lightwood," or kindling, that fuels a swiftly growing fire. For Judah, the breaking point is his father's indifference when the Scorpions brutally maim his little brother Benji. Sherwood's refusal to visit Benji in the hospital or retaliate against the Scorpions—he orders Judah to "lay low" and "think about the cash at stake"—finally motivates Judah to turn on his father, take his fate into his own hands, and attempt to redefine the Cannon name (144).

In this violent and poverty-stricken world, no one has the luxury of making mistakes with impunity. At the same time, the right path is far from clear, and the wrong choice can have devastating consequences. The only character who seems not to accept the possibility of failure is Tulah, a power-hungry, manipulative Pentecostal preacher who uses her influence to fortify her own wealth and prestige. She is a materialistic, arrogant hypocrite, but she truly believes in her power, and others do too; she has her congregation and even the entire town under her thumb. Tulah proves to be the villain that *A Tree Born Crooked* lacked, a force of evil who provides impetus to the plot and raises the stakes—anyone who crosses her will certainly pay. However, even Tulah cannot entirely escape the repercussions of her continual machinations. In an O'Connor-esque moment toward the end of the novel, Sherwood gouges out one of Tulah's eyes, symbolizing her moral blindness and demonstrating that no one is invulnerable.

Walk in the Fire explores the aftermath of *Lightwood*'s cataclysmic conclusion and probes the psychology and complex motivations of these characters that too often lurk at the fringes of the narrative as leering, one-dimensional villains. Judah now runs the Cannon criminal operation after Sherwood's death, and we could easily imagine him appearing for a couple of minutes in another story as just a macho, drug-dealing thug with no brains to speak of. Here Post lays bare his inner struggle, the forces that conspire to keep him an outcast from the rest of society despite his best intentions, and the steady rise of his darker side. Judah is in many ways a victim of circumstance, but Ramey repeatedly insists that he also has agency and can break free from the cycle of violence if he chooses. We may sympathize with Judah, but we do not pity him as we would a helpless child; with Ramey, we see "the lurking, hulking hydra of ambition and hubris, of penitence and doubt, coiling itself around his heart" (102). He first accepts his father's position unwillingly, but after the first taste of power, a craving to stay king of the Cannon kingdom slowly worms its way into his heart, pushing even Ramey aside. Judah falls into the same trap as Tulah: he wants "to be king of the mountain," to wield his power without penalty, "to walk in the fire and not be burned" (165).

Judah's overwhelming loyalty to his family and his love for Ramey prevent him from becoming the monster he fears, but Post is not afraid to explore the blacker side of humanity through depraved characters who have no redeeming qualities. *Walk in the Fire* introduces Weaver, who kills nonchalantly, just for sport, and is a villain more in the mode of McCarthy, "led by the wasteland inside him and his pure disregard for human life" (280). Tulah is still a force of malevolence to be reckoned with, but in this novel she becomes more like O'Connor's self-righteous, idiosyncratic villains. Even in the midst of a terrifying religious ceremony called the Recompense, which takes place at the dead of night in a forest and involves masked participants, drinking of poison, and sometimes outright slaying of its members, Tulah herself usually seems more eccentric and conceited than demonic. In an almost comical manner reminiscent of Ruby Turpin in O'Connor's short story "Revelation," Tulah peers curiously through her mask at everyone else in an attempt to quickly calculate her rank in the hierarchy: "She couldn't see who was beside her in her own row, but she was pleased to be standing even with the Flaming Sword. Her rank had most certainly improved this year" (237).

Tulah's religion proves to be disturbing and perhaps more Satanic than truly Pentecostal, but it is never inauthentic. Indeed, authenticity is one of Post's hallmarks. Everything about her writing is genuine, from the characters to the smallest, seemingly insignificant details. At one point in *Walk in the Fire*, Judah finds himself with a Parliament cigarette in his hand and wonders what has happened to him: "Who the hell smoked p-funks?" (73–74). Only someone intimately familiar with this culture would know that Parliaments are derisively called "p-funks." The bar scenes in particular always ring utterly true to life, and the novel's occasional bits of humor are spot on: "You'd be surprised at how many people come here looking for the strip club," the owner of a fish and pet store tells Judah. "I do half my business that way. They come through the door looking for pussy, but they leave with a goldfish. The goldfish ain't on sale today, though" (116). All of Post's work features this kind of detail, but *Walk in the Fire* moves at a more deliberate yet insistent pace that gives Post time to showcase her knowledge of her material and delve into more detail about the world and the characters who inhabit it.

Walk in the Fire also allows Post to flesh out relatively minor characters and offer them room to grow. Her treatment of Felton in particular is an achievement. It is one thing to paint a complex and sympathetic portrait of Judah and Ramey, two independent and lawless "badasses" whom we might admire as true-blooded Americans taking destiny into their own hands. It is another matter entirely to create a compassionate and interesting depiction of someone like Felton, Tulah's apparently spineless, simpering nephew. But Felton comes into his own in this novel, gains the courage to "look his aunt in her one, pale, remaining eye and not give in," and even experiences true religious visions and inspirations that are as real as Tulah's (29). In fact, Tulah's vision at the Recompense may well prophesy Felton's ascendency and her own demise: she sees a crow fly toward her through a red sky and land on the branch of a dead tree, which turns to ash beneath the bird's "spindly feet" (240).

Tulah may be the dead tree that will soon be ash, but if she will burn, so too will the Cannons and Ramey; all of them have decided to walk in the fire, and all of them know that they cannot walk forever without being burned. By the end, even Ramey, whose sense of right and wrong seems most stalwart, feels as if they have crossed a line from which there is no turning back: "A sharpness stole into Ramey's heart, at once thrilling and terrifying. It was sealed; things would never be the same" (311). They have killed and they have conquered for the moment, but Tulah's wrath is about to descend in the last installment of what Post has said will be a trilogy: "She would steal the last breath from each and every one of them and they would all ride the pale horse home. . . . It was time to reap what had been sown" (313). Again, in this world, characters cannot escape the consequences of their mistakes, no matter how well intentioned. Soon they will reap what they have sown, and no doubt some "shall lie down in sorrow" in the next chapter of the Cannon saga, as Isaiah 50:11 promises in the novel's epigraph.

In retrospect, this ominous verse from Isaiah would not be out of place at the beginning of any of Post's novels—a fact Post acknowledges and embraces: "Dennis Lehane once famously called the Noir genre (one I identify with even more than the broad 'crime' label) 'working class tragedy' and I think that definition really encompasses what I write" ("'Lightwood' Author Steph Post"). The growth Post has shown over the course of her first three novels, as well as the speed with which she has published them, suggests that her voice will continue to rise among authors of the Rough South and that she has more to show us about how noir intersects with the Rough South.

Works Cited

Bancroft, Colette. "Review: Local Author Steph Post Takes Readers on a Twisted Ride in 'Lightwood.'" *Tampa Bay Times*, January 19, 2017. https://www.tampabay.com/features

/books/review-local-author-steph-post-takes-readers-on-a-twisted-ride-in-lightwood
/2310074. Accessed October 13, 2018.

Catalano, Kevin. "A Conversation with Steph Post." *Coil Magazine*, December 27, 2017. https://
medium.com/the-coil/steph-post-interview-by-kevin-catalano-1c0c3a7c957d. Accessed
September 14, 2018.

Lauden, S. W. "Interrogation—Steph Post." BadCitizenCorporation.com, February 13, 2017.
https://badcitizencorporation.com/2017/02/13/interrogation-steph-post. Accessed
September 12, 2018.

Post, Steph. "A Conversation with Steph Post." Interview with Kevin Catalano. *Coil Magazine*,
December 27, 2017. https://medium.com/the-coil/steph-post-interview-by-kevin-catalano
-1c0c3a7c957d. Accessed September 14, 2018.

Post, Steph. *A Tree Born Crooked*. Polis Books, 2014.

Post, Steph. *Lightwood*. Polis Books, 2017.

Post, Steph. "'Lightwood' Author Steph Post: The LCG Lounge Interview." *La Casita Grande*,
October 12, 2018. https://www.lcgeditores.com/blog/2018/2/20/lightwood-author-steph
-post-the-lcg-lounge-interview. Accessed September 6, 2018.

Post, Steph. *Miraculum*. Polis Books, 2019.

Post, Steph. *Walk in the Fire*. Polis Books, 2018.

Thomas Pierce, born in South Carolina in 1982, is the author of a novel, *The Afterlives*, and a short story collection, *Hall of Small Mammals*, for which he was honored with the National Book Foundation's 5 Under 35 Award. He holds an MFA from the University of Virginia, where he was a Poe/Faulkner Fellow. His stories have appeared in the *New Yorker*, *Atlantic*, *Zoetrope*, *Oxford American*, and *Virginia Quarterly Review* and have been anthologized in *The Best American Non-required Reading* and *O. Henry Prize Stories*. He has reported for *NPR* and *National Geographic Magazine*. He lives outside Charlottesville, Virginia, with his wife and daughters.

"The Right Place for Love"
The Fiction of Thomas Pierce

Richard Gaughran

The fiction of Thomas Pierce takes place in an American South in transition, a landscape in which collard greens and fried chicken compete with flax-seed pancakes and whole-wheat spaghetti with black-bean meatballs. As Pierce has remarked in a 2015 interview, "If I'm writing about a character at dinner, maybe I shouldn't put him at a meat-and-three but at the Applebee's or a Thai restaurant. Maybe a character has a Robert E. Lee portrait over her mantel but maybe she also goes to hatha yoga classes every morning and drinks iced almond-milk lattes or whatever" ("Inventing Situations").

Pierce's southerners now have the internet, access to a wide, sometimes strange world, where they constantly confront new ideas and new theories about the world, some of them based on sound science, some decidedly suspect. Pierce's South, as he has said, is "a culture in conflict with itself" ("Inventing Situations"). To heighten the sense that the ground under human life is constantly shifting, Pierce sets much of his fiction a little bit into the future. For instance, in his story "Shirley Temple Three," the technology of cloning has advanced beyond current practice, so that prehistoric creatures are "resurrected." In other stories, travel to other planets is possible. In his debut novel, *The Afterlives* (2018), historical figures are brought back to life as holograms, and living individuals are replicated, so that a hologram of a famous football player stands outside a food chain to entice passersby to enter; a famous actress, or so it appears, models bracelets in a jewelry store.

Pierce possesses a fertile imagination. "I've always enjoyed making things up," he says (interview with the author). In his fiction, he has created fictional worlds that require characters to confront their confusions and readjust their thinking about ultimate meanings. What is the nature of reality? Why are we here? Is there a world beyond the material one? Is death the end or a new beginning? A half century before Pierce, another southern writer, Flannery O'Connor, famously remarked that the South as she knew it was "Christ-haunted," though not "Christ-centered" (818). In the same lecture, "Some Aspects of the Grotesque in Southern Fiction," O'Connor asserted, with some qualification, that "in the South the general conception of man is still, in the main, theological" (817). The fiction of the South, she concluded, is necessarily concerned with "mystery and the unexpected" (815). Although Pierce has expressed admiration for O'Connor's work, he is no O'Connor imitator. O'Connor never ventures into what might be considered science fiction, for instance. Yet Pierce shares with O'Connor the concern for ultimate meanings, for metaphysical query, for mystery. His characters, however, often labor to discern these vital meanings in a new context, one in which new technologies arrive continually, in which new knowledge confronts traditional custom and belief. Pierce has been straightforward in describing this constant in his work:

> I'm drawn to characters who are asking questions about their existence and who are trying to explain the universe to themselves. The ways in which people come up with their explanations, typically, involve some combination of science and religion. Those are two avenues of investigation available to us when it comes to understanding who we are and how we got here. Many of these stories take place at moments when a character's beliefs—about Creation, about the soul, about a relationship, et al.—are being tested by a new technological development or by a mysterious skull or a strange dream. The characters have to reevaluate those beliefs and, more often than not, adapt. ("A 'Slightly Askew Universe'")

"Shirley Temple Three," the first story in Pierce's debut collection, *Hall of Small Mammals* (2014), dramatizes this dynamic with humor and insight. The premise is simple, though startlingly inventive: Tommy, the careless son of the main character, called Mawmaw in the story, works for a television show that profiles a recently cloned prehistoric creature in each episode. The cloning is governed by rules, one of which requires that one of a pair of accidental twins must be euthanized rather than transported to a special zoo. A creature called a Bread Island Dwarf Mammoth is one such twin, which Tommy, flouting the rules, smuggles into his Mawmaw's home. Left alone for months with the cloned mammoth, named Shirley Temple Three, Mawmaw wonders how to care for the creature: What does it eat? Why is it shedding? How can it survive in the hot, humid weather? Mostly, however, as a member of a traditional Christian church called God's Sacred Light, she wonders about the moral propriety of bringing such creatures to life. She has seemingly made an intellectual accommodation, or rationalization, concerning the book of Genesis and its six days of creation. Those days are not twenty-four-hour periods, as some strict literalists would have it, but God's days, each of which "might have been a million years long" (11). So, yes, there was an era in which dinosaurs roamed. However, her moral questions linger, for Shirley Temple Three has "been yanked out of its own time and lives outside God's natural laws" (11).

It is the practice in Mawmaw's culture, and in her personal experience, to bring moral and theological concerns to a spiritual guide. So, especially after Shirley Temple Three shows signs of illness, Mawmaw calls on the leader of her congregation, Pastor Frank. The minister makes a house call and, while drinking his decaffeinated tea, disapprovingly mentions the show for which Tommy works. Pastor Frank admits he has never seen the show, but he has heard rumors, one of which claims that the show has brought back a Neanderthal. Rather than listen to Mawmaw's clarifications, he launches into dogma. He says there are two possibilities with the science of cloning: either beings from the past—Neanderthals, in the pastor's example—were purposely eliminated by God, and therefore cloning violates God's will, or such creatures never existed, the fossil record having been planted by the Devil (23). After hearing the pastor's inflexible analysis, Mawmaw remains quiet about the miniature mammoth and simply asks the pastor to pray for her son, and also for what she calls her ailing "dog."

Mawmaw's questions concerning the morality of cloning remain unanswered. Instead Pierce's story leaves the reader with an understanding of a sympathetic character, and it leaves that character with an experience that disrupts her habitual loneliness and brings out her capacity for nurturing. At story's end, Shirley Temple Three is loose in the neighborhood somewhere, for which

Mawmaw is grateful when Tommy reappears with the intention of eliminating the creature. She is sure the creature will return once Tommy leaves, and she tellingly refers to the place of that return as Shirley's "home" (28).

Pierce's "Shirley Temple Three" establishes a thematic pattern in the writer's work. In challenging a character's customary understanding of the universe, the story does not allow for a retreat to tradition. On the other hand, neither does its main character's new perspective entail replacing traditional understandings with an uncritical embrace of technological innovation. Rather, Mawmaw expresses universal human values that arise naturally from experience—concern, nurturing, love—values dependent neither on religious dogma nor on scientific rationalism and certainty.

The characters in Pierce's fiction are defined by their searches for meaning. They yearn for answers, or *the* answer. The traditions of Protestantism linger in their memories, and sometimes in their habits, but they are less committed to these ways of thinking than they might have been in a previous generation. They investigate new lines of thinking but still long for the security, the blessed assurance, of the born-again. In his futuristic fictions, Pierce places his characters on the road, so to speak, as though they are new versions of John Bunyan's Christian, journeying toward the Celestial City—or so they hope. A 2017 story that appeared in the *New Yorker*, "Chairman Spaceman," provides another variation on this theme, again denying the protagonist "the answer," or at least not in the terms he expected.

The title of "Chairman Spaceman" refers to the main character, Dom Whipple. The moniker is playfully bestowed on him by his acquaintance and fellow church member Jerome, for Dom is preparing to relocate to a planet chosen by their church, called "God's Plan for Space," not coincidentally abbreviated "GPS": "God's Plan had a simple mission—to establish a more egalitarian society on another planet and to spread the message of God's love to unexplored solar systems" (69). Dom has been a ruthless businessman, a corporate raider known as the "layoff king" (69). But after ruining his marriage, he declares himself a changed man and donates all his earthly goods to God's Plan, in exchange for which he will join others in populating a small, distant planet, which Dom imagines as a kind of heaven. After being frozen for several decades, he will awaken on this utopia, literally born again. But wary readers suspect something is not right, especially when the narrator takes them inside Dom's condescending thoughts as he bids farewell to his acquaintances and his ex-wife, Nona. Dom imagines that when he wakes on the new planet, he will still be young and vigorous, while those left behind will have aged after struggling through their confusing lives on Earth: "He tried not to feel bad for them, these future old geezers in this grimy kitchen, on this miserable planet, making the best of it, muddling through their lives without attempting anything big or monumental" (71).

Dom insists on what he calls his chance at "a fresh start," and in this impulse he mirrors numerous other characters from American fiction, whether Huckleberry Finn, Jay Gatsby, or Thomas Sutpen. To be sure, the country itself was founded by immigrants eager for a fresh start, and the impulse to seek new frontiers while attempting to erase the past is deeply rooted in the American psyche, as numerous observers have noted. This predisposition has been encouraged and given particular expression by the Transcendentalists, thinkers such as Emerson and Thoreau, who argued for a stripping away of illusion and the creation of a purified, simplified self, one able to apprehend higher Truth. Dom is on such a quest, but Pierce's story ends in bitter irony. After being frozen for thirty years, Dom is awakened and told the mission had to be aborted and the ship returned to Earth, because the target planet turned out to be less hospitable than thought—not a utopia after all. He is greeted by Nona, now an aged woman embarrassed to be seen by this still youthful man, and she informs him that family members and acquaintances have died. Dom escaped the everydayness of life, but at what price? Rather than achieving something "big and monumental," he has slept through life. He has certainly not even heeded his father's words, delivered in a parting toast on the night before he boarded his spaceship: "All I ask . . . is that you remember us. When you're standing on some very foreign shore, don't forget to gaze up into the night sky sometimes and think about your parents and your friends, all the people who loved you here on earth, regardless" (73).

The words of Dom's father bear traces of Robert Frost's "Birches," a poem that takes a skeptical view of transcendental pursuit, settling instead for what is known through lived experience: "Earth's the right place for love: / I don't know where it's likely to go better." Indeed, Pierce's story makes it clear that love still exists between Dom and Nona. Despite her misgivings, she is the one to greet him after thirty years, and they make love before his departure, a scene that ends with Dom sobbing into Nona's chest. Furthermore, in the hours before he leaves Earth, he becomes acutely aware of the real presence of the smallest things: the feel of a paper cup against his teeth, the smell of exhaust in heavy traffic. The narrator says he "marveled at the world he was soon to leave behind" (71). Despite these feelings, Dom allows his obsession to consume him, so he follows his church's teachings to the letter, forsaking all possessions, even to the point of having to enter the spaceship naked. He has stripped himself down to nothing and achieved nothing, rather than face the earthly "muddle" in which others struggle, rather than confront whatever human foibles and failures are embedded in the "regardless" of his father's toast. As Pierce himself has said in reference to "Chairman Spaceman," "I believe that our fate, as a species, is tied to the fate of the Earth. We are accountable to it and to each other" ("Thomas Pierce on an Anti-escapist Adventure").

Pierce has not, to my knowledge, referred to the Frost poem in connection with his fiction, but in a note at the end of his *Hall of Small Mammals*, he mentions the significance of another poet, Theodore Roethke, specifically his "In a Dark Time," first published in 1960. The poem's rich imagery chronicles the speaker's psychic crisis, a disintegration of the self, asking in the last of its four stanzas, "Which I is *I*?" But the lines that follow, and end the poem, suggest a reunification of the self, though the victory is mitigated by an acknowledgment that the world does not offer up easy answers:

A fallen man, I climb out of my fear.
The mind enters itself, and God the mind,
And one is One, free in the tearing wind.

Pierce's note at the end of his story collection appears to be a simple acknowledgment that a line from "Grasshopper Kings," the third story in *Hall of Small Mammals*, was borrowed from Roethke. The story refers to an organization, the Grasshoppers, a kind of club for gradually revealing "truths" to young people, and it chronicles a father and son attending a Grasshopper Camp, where the father, Flynn, feels generally mystified by the proceedings, and by his relationship to his son, and he wonders what these "truths" might be. Another father in attendance has cajoled his own son into revealing "the First Truth," which he repeats to Flynn, though neither man understands it. It is the paraphrase of Roethke, "*Let the mind enter itself*" (73). But Pierce, in acknowledging his borrowing, adds something else, saying that Roethke's entire poem "could have served as an epigraph to this collection" (294). Pierce is referring to the compatibility of his themes to those in Roethke's poem. In an interview with the *New Yorker*, given just before the publication of *Hall of Small Mammals*, Pierce says, "I think what interests me are situations in which people have to let go of something—a self, an idea, a history, a belief, a system of thought, a desire, a relationship—in order to confront the world as it is, or, maybe, even to see beyond the world as it is." He then notes that he puts his characters in "dark" situations because, from the depths, "the eye begins to see" ("This Week in Fiction"), quoting from the first line of Roethke's poem: "In a dark time, the eye begins to see."

This theme, which arises in almost every story in *Hall of Small Mammals*, also emerges in Pierce's debut novel, *The Afterlives* (2018). The main character, Jim Byrd, has experienced "a dark time." Specifically, at age thirty-three, his heart stopped beating for several minutes; technically he died. The experience left him with no knowledge about an immaterial world, so he embarks on an anxious metaphysical search. At one point, he explains himself to a hypnotherapist: "I was here and then I wasn't. . . . God didn't show himself to me. No feelings of ecstasy. No paradise. And I do not find this idea peaceful" (211). He feels as though he is treading into an abyss: "I feel like we're all marching toward the edge of a cliff. It's beautiful, sure, from a distance, but once your feet are at the edge, it's just a giant freaking hole" (211). This passage also echoes Roethke's poem, where the speaker says, as he teeters on the edge of sanity, "The edge is what I have."

In *The Afterlives*, Pierce's characters have replaced traditional faith with a trust in technological innovation, a trust encouraged by corporate entities. Byrd himself wears a device called HeartNet, a kind of defibrillator in constant contact with the parent company in California. He also starts attending a new kind of church, the Church of Search, which lacks a traditional creed, its services consisting of lectures, often delivered by holograms that more often than not argue that ultimate answers are near at hand, that technology will show the way. One proponent of the church, Wesley Riggs, insists that death itself is on the verge of being defeated: "People don't die anymore, they just fail to find the right cure. We're more fortunate than anyone who's come before us. Because we're so close to having all the answers. We're at the cusp of a new era" (57). Jim Byrd envies his friend's confidence and tries to find such assurance for himself. He says of Wesley, "He didn't need God or the afterlife, not when he had accelerators and scanners. Maybe he was right" (222).

The bulk of Pierce's novel chronicles a series of Byrd's searches as he experiments with various technologies and consults various "experts," all in an attempt to answer a question about life and death that traditional

Christianity had once settled. And he is joined in this quest by Anne, someone who reenters his life several years after she lost her husband to a mysterious drowning. They fall in love and eventually marry, and together they attempt to communicate with the dead—in an old house where there was once a deadly fire, through hypnotism, or in consultation with a fortune-teller. Byrd finally tracks down a paranormal researcher, Sally Zinker, who has invented something called the "Reunion Machine," which she claims can connect the living with the dead. Byrd tells her about his recently deceased father, hoping he will be able to talk with him, and he succinctly explains why: "I just want to know if this is it, if I'm going to disappear when I die" (252). Anne is also interested in a session with the Reunion Machine, hoping to connect with her first husband. After some negotiation with Sally Zinker, they are each separately connected to the machine. Both experience something profound, but afterward they aren't sure whether they entered a spiritual dimension or whether the machine merely enhanced their memories and fantasies (307). Even the inventor cannot be sure: "I'll never be able to prove beyond a shadow of a doubt that the machine is doing what I say it can do" (327).

A short summary cannot account for the complexities of *The Afterlives*. It contains considerable humor, for one thing, and also includes some shifts in literary point of view, with short interchapters that contain nonchronological narrative fragments. As for the main characters' central search, the answer remains elusive. Sally Zinker can never verify what her machine does. Byrd later learns that she died while using it. Byrd's father's statement is no doubt the novel's answer to the reader looking for knowledge about a spiritual dimension: "At a certain point, you either trust that there's more than meets the eye—or you don't" (177). Pierce himself has made a similarly tentative remark in a radio interview upon the novel's release: "I'm very open to things that are not explained, and I just have a hard time believing that this material universe is all there is" ("In 'The Afterlives'").

At the end of *The Afterlives*, Jim and Anne leave behind their search: "Out of necessity we had to move forward with our lives. There were diapers to change, fruits to puree, a baby to rock and get back to sleep in the middle of the night" (355–56). Byrd decides that a single phrase summarizes our lives: "a grand complication" (349). After forsaking his search and "climbing out of his fear," to paraphrase Roethke's important poem, Byrd is able to embrace the world and its tangible splendors: "There were beautiful spring mornings, the azalea bushes and pear trees blossoming pink and white up and down the street, the Blue Ridge Mountains hazy and beautiful out beyond the tree line" (356). More importantly, he experiences love, specifically with Anne. In the novel's last lines, he feels his flawed heart beating unevenly and becomes anxious, but then his wife arrives: "I was going to be all right. I opened my eyes, and, thank God, there she was" (366). To return to Robert Frost's line, "Earth's the right place for love."

Pierce's novel, and his fiction in general, does not scoff at these searchers. Sally Zinker dies using her Reunion Machine, to be sure, but Pierce's tone lacks disapproval. He has said, "I don't think of myself as a particularly ironic writer," going so far as to say, "I'd like to see a world where that machine is available to lots of people" (interview with the author). The searches undertaken by Pierce's characters, whether in his stories or in his first novel, remain mysterious and often inconclusive, yet the search is always worth it; and characters, like Jim and Anne Byrd, find their lives enriched by the experience. Such literature has the capacity to open readers to a similar sense of wonder.

Works Cited

Frost, Robert. "Birches." In Collected Poems, Prose and Plays, 117–18. Library of America, 1995.

O'Connor, Flannery. "Some Aspects of the Grotesque in Southern Fiction." In Collected Works, 813–21. Library of America, 1988.

Pierce, Thomas. The Afterlives. Riverhead, 2018.

Pierce, Thomas. "Chairman Spaceman." New Yorker, January 16, 2017, 68–75.

Pierce, Thomas. "Grasshopper Kings." In Hall of Small Mammals, by Thomas Pierce, 55–83. Riverhead, 2014.

Pierce, Thomas. "In 'The Afterlives,' Holograms and Ghosts Give Meaning to Life after Death." Interview with Rachel Martin. Morning Edition (NPR), February 5, 2018. https://www.npr .org/2018/02/05/582377232/in-the-afterlives-holograms-and-ghosts-give-meaning-to-life -after-death. Accessed July 25, 2018.

Pierce, Thomas. "Inventing Situations: An Interview with Thomas Pierce." Interview with James Yeh. Paris Review, January 8, 2015. https://www.theparisreview.org/blog/2015/01/08 /inventing-situations-an-interview-with-thomas-pierce. Accessed July 25, 2018.

Pierce, Thomas. Interview with the author. September 26, 2018.

Pierce, Thomas. "Shirley Temple Three." In Hall of Small Mammals, by Thomas Pierce, 1–28. Riverhead, 2014.

Pierce, Thomas. "A 'Slightly Askew Universe': In Conversation with Thomas Pierce." Interview with Corinne Gould. Late Night Library, January 26, 2015. https://latenightlibrary.org /thomas-pierce. Accessed July 25, 2018.

Pierce, Thomas. "This Week in Fiction: Thomas Pierce." Interview with Cressida Leyshon. New Yorker, May 23, 2014. https://www.newyorker.com/books/page-turner/this-week-in-fiction -thomas-pierce. Accessed July 25, 2018.

Pierce, Thomas. "Thomas Pierce on an Anti-escapist Space Adventure." Interview with Cressida Leyshon. *New Yorker*, January 9, 2017. https://www.newyorker.com/books/page-turner/fiction-this-week-thomas-pierce-2017-01-16. Accessed July 25, 2018.

Roethke, Theodore. "In a Dark Time." In *Selected Poems*, edited by Edward Hirsch, 116. Library of America, 2005.

Taylor Brown was born in Brunswick, Georgia, in 1982 and grew up in the resort community of St. Simons Island, where his father, Rick Brown, was a founding partner in a local law firm. Brown majored in English at the University of Georgia in Athens, where he graduated in 2005; his first published short fiction appeared in 2008. He has lived as an adult in Buenos Aires, San Francisco, and Asheville, North Carolina; he currently resides in Wilmington, where he manages an internet marketing firm he founded, Bikebound. com. Rick Brown, who shared Taylor's enthusiasm for motorcycles, was a contributor to the site until his death in a riding accident in 2017. Taylor's most recent publications include firsthand accounts of Hurricane Florence's September 2018 Wilmington landfall, published in the Charleston-based *Garden & Gun*, and in the *New York Times*. He is the author of the story collection *In the Season of Blood & Gold* (2014) and four novels: *Fallen Land* (2015), *The River of Kings* (2017), *Gods of Howl Mountain* (2018), and *Pride of Eden* (2020).

Landscapes of Blood and Desire
The Fiction of Taylor Brown

Shawn E. Miller

Now in his mid-thirties, the novelist Taylor Brown is still at the beginning of what many expect will be a prolific career. He began publishing stories in literary reviews in 2008, a few years after graduating from the University of Georgia; in 2014, ten of those stories, along with two previously unpublished, were collected in his first book, *In the Season of Blood & Gold*. Since then, he has published four novels in quick succession, all set in the American South, and all concerned in one way or another with the American past. For southern writers, the past has traditionally meant a focus on the Civil War, and the war is, in fact, the backdrop of Brown's first novel, *Fallen Land*, published in 2015. In his third novel, *Gods of Howl Mountain* (2018), his canvas includes 1950s moonshining and nascent NASCAR in the North Carolina highlands after a wounded veteran's return from the Korean War. But nowhere is Brown's preoccupation with history more plain than in his 2017 novel, *The River of Kings*, which encompasses three distinct yet presumably related narrative threads: the present-day journey of two brothers down the Altamaha River in Georgia to scatter their father's ashes, that father's adult life along the same river from 1975 to 2001, and, most strikingly, the brief but dramatic establishment and occupation of the French Fort Caroline in the New World from 1564 to 1565. All three narratives occupy the same geography, suggesting an ability of landscape to shape human desire, and to make stories of that desire, across centuries.

Brown's first book, the story collection *In the Season of Blood & Gold*, is remarkable for the range it exhibits, and the stories are so different from one another that generalizing about the collection is difficult. It begins with the award-winning story "Rider," which is narrated with all the hallmarks of a fable: no character names, only pronouns and a few vague identifiers like "the rider," "the widow," and "the warden"; no identifiable geography; and no anchor in history—all told in a style owing much to Cormac McCarthy at his most self-indulgent. No other story in the collection is like it. Some of the others concern domestic themes in clearly contemporary settings, as in "The Tattooist's Daughter," which is about a young woman's difficult relationship with her mother. Others cover a historical period from the Civil War—as in the collection's finale and title piece, "In the Season of Blood & Gold"—to the postapocalyptic, dystopian future evoked in "Sin-Eaters." One commonality among most of the stories is an earnest and tenderhearted sentimentalism conveyed whenever Brown puts a sympathetic secondary character in a perilous circumstance. Such figures are common in the collection: a young widow living alone in the woods ("Rider"), a little girl attacked by an alligator ("Bone Valley"), an abused dog ("The Vizsla"), a newborn orphaned in a dying world ("Sin-Eaters"), a wounded veteran ("Home Guard"), a boy's dead mother ("Covered Bridge"), a young woman about to be raped by Confederate raiders ("In the Season of Blood & Gold").

The collection's variety suggests a young writer casting about for a characteristic voice and mode; it also indicates the remarkable breadth of Brown's ability at the beginning of his career. Short fiction has so far been the source of all his novels, and two have their genesis here: the title piece, largely unaltered, became the first chapter of Brown's first novel, the Civil War romance *Fallen Land*, in 2015. And Brown's third novel, *Gods of Howl Mountain*, owes its fictional world, as well as some early imagery and language, to the story "Kingdom Come." The collection also marked a beginning for Brown in the sense that its strength got him noticed. *In the Season of Blood & Gold* was released by a small Winston-Salem publisher, Press 53, which had existed fewer than ten years at the time. The book attracted the interest of the much larger and well-established St. Martin's Press, which has published all of Brown's subsequent novels.

Brown's second novel, *The River of Kings*, provides a useful lens through which to view the interplay of history, landscape, and desire in his fiction more generally. The impetus for the novel was a river float trip Brown had taken with college buddies when he was twenty-one. He has written about this trip in essays published in *Salt Magazine* ("Along the Little Amazon," January 2017) and *Garden & Gun* ("Georgia's Little Amazon," February–March 2018). He had originally fictionalized it in the story "Riverkeepers," which appeared in the literary journal *Chautauqua* in 2015.

The novel's structure is easily Brown's most experimental and formally interesting. The action takes place in three narrative threads at different points in history. In the present, two brothers kayak down the Altamaha River in Georgia over five days. They carry their recently deceased father's ashes, which they mean to scatter near the sea. The elder brother, Lawton, is a Navy SEAL; the younger, Hunter, is an English major at the University of Georgia and, as Brown has hinted, a version of Brown himself. Meanwhile, from 1975 to 2001, the father whose ashes they carry struggles to make a living, support a family, and perhaps realize much wilder dreams, on the same river. While the relationship between these two narratives seems obvious enough, we might struggle to connect them to the third, which is set in the sixteenth century and concerns the French colonial experience at Fort Caroline, again on the Altamaha. In this story, which Brown researched meticulously, we are with the historical French artist Jacques Le Moyne, whose engravings serve as the book's illustrations and adorn its endpapers, as he documents an early European sojourn in North America, emphasizing the colonists' conflicts with natives, with the Spanish, and among themselves. None of the three stories is narrated in retrospect, and they develop independently of one another, with chapter titles designating place and time, as in "Altamaha River, Day 1," "New France, June 1564," and "Darien, Georgia, 1982." Additionally, the novel is divided into three books with narrative epigraphs in which we are with a mysterious old man doing and thinking odd things; eventually we realize the man is Uncle King, a charismatic preacher-prophet who appears in the two latter-day narratives.

That the latter-day narratives rub up against the colonial narrative in the same novel suggests that all three are related, but how they are related, and especially what the Fort Caroline material has to do with much more recent events, seems cloudy. Brown is careful, however, to emphasize phenomena that occur across all three. Most plainly, they share a geography: the Altamaha

River as it winds its way to the Georgia coast. This geography predates even the French, a feature that is also true of some of the other motifs Brown uses to signal relationship: the ancient cypress trees the brothers find along their route that were already giants when Le Moyne sketched them in 1564; the migration of sturgeon, a constant since the Triassic Period; the megalodon tooth Hunter wears around his neck that, the text hints, may be the same "tongue stone" Le Moyne finds and later throws back into the river "for another hand or foot to find" (311), and may indicate a sympathy between the two characters as artist-documentarians; and, most curiously, the enduring mythology of a Loch Ness Monster–style creature lurking in the depths of the river, the so-called Altamaha-ha. Le Moyne and the French encounter the creature, which is well-known to the natives, as soon as they begin to navigate the river; it appears to be "leading them" (11). Even in the present, the Altamaha-ha is a subject of reflection between the brothers, and it is the beast the enigmatic Uncle King hunts.

As the river endures across centuries, so does the way men regard it. For the French, the river promises—falsely, as it turns out—to deliver them to a land laden with gold and riches like those seized by Spanish conquistadores much farther south. While the natives have no interest in gold, Brown does not suggest they are really all that different from their European guests; they have their own notions of what is upriver and desire it as keenly, tempting the French with tales of gold to enlist their arquebuses to native ends. The promise of fulfilled desire is likewise what drives the brothers' father, Hiram Loggins, up and down the banks of the Altamaha. He makes his living as a shrimper, but he turns to fishing for "square grouper" (smuggled marijuana bales dropped into the water by aircraft), and eventually to illegal harvesting of endangered sturgeon roe, prized as caviar. While the details are murky, the latter enterprise assuredly gets him killed. This is, perhaps, what Brown suggests with the putative river monster: the creature represents human desire provoked and whetted by landscape and grown monstrous, resulting, in both narratives of the past, in misery and death.

This ability of landscape to endure, and to provoke, shape, and often thwart human desire, is characteristic of Brown's approach to the American past throughout his work. When we consider his novels together, we can also add that Brown seems interested not merely in the well-worn great upheavals typical of historical fiction, but also in more subtle transitions in times of economic and social change. Even Brown's first novel, *Fallen Land,* though it is set against the backdrop of the Civil War, concentrates on the margins of that event: the guerrilla war in the mountains of Virginia, North Carolina, and Tennessee, and the aftermath of Sherman's march to the sea. Here we find a world of irregulars and raiders of questionable loyalties where peacetime checks on human behavior have been loosened, a world much like that of the Kansas-Missouri border wars rendered in Daniel Woodrell's *Woe to Live On*, a comparison Brown has himself made. The novel's protagonists, Callum and Ava, are both in a sense orphans. As Brown has recounted in the Literary Hub essay "How I Accidentally Wrote a Civil War Novel" (2016), he drew inspiration for the original short story from the traditional folk ballad "When First unto This Country," about an immigrant who steals a horse to ride to his love. Like the voice in the song, Callum is an immigrant; his parents died of hanging and typhus in the old country, and his foster family carried him to America as a child before they perished of yellow fever. His second foster father, lately his comrade in arms, has joined a posse led by a vicious, one-armed slave hunter who pursues the couple relentlessly. Ava's orphanhood is a more recent consequence of the war. The pair's story is one of comedy discovered in the midst of tragedy: war brings them together, and their flight from violence and death points these orphans toward home, marriage, and family.

Brown's other historical settings are less dramatic than a great war or the European conquest of the Americas; still, they are always set in times of transition. That is certainly true of Hiram Loggins's world of changing economic conditions in *The River of Kings*, as it is of the 1950s North Carolina highlands we encounter in *Gods of Howl Mountain*. Here is a world rooted in the past, like its female lead, Granny May, who is a practitioner of traditional herbal medicine, and like the magnificent American chestnut that looms over her yard, a specimen by that time so rare that the University of North Carolina sends a couple of biologists to study it, hoping that the secret of its resistance to chestnut blight can help save the species. Yet, as the anachronistic tree suggests, the world of the novel's present is already a product of transition that has, in some cases, altered the landscape itself, as the first chapter foregrounds: TVA flooding has swallowed a populated valley and changed the contours of Gumtree, North Carolina, creating a marginal section of town, characterized by seedy nightclubs and whorehouses, called End-of-the-Road because here the road runs straight into the man-made lake. And in the present, transition is ongoing, with implications for Granny

May's isolated and ungovernable mountain community, which owes its economy to distilling and smuggling moonshine, a trade that her grandson Rory Docherty finds increasingly difficult to carry on. This transition will, readers know in hindsight, repeat itself even after Granny May and Rory have managed to supplant moonshining with marijuana cultivation. As in *The River of Kings*, an enduring landscape plants the seeds of human desire and determines its course. Landscape tempts that desire to outgrow its bounds, as it had with the French, as it does with Hiram Loggins, and as it does with this novel's monster, the ruthless moonshiner and gang lord Eustace Graham.

Brown's recently published fourth novel *Pride of Eden* (2020) seems a departure from some of these themes. Like his prior novels, this one began as short fiction, specifically in two stories, "Rhino Girl" and "The Lioness," both published in 2016. In the novel's main action, Malaya of "Rhino Girl," a third-generation Filipino American who grew up in Georgia, joined the military, and has worked as a park ranger in South Africa, joins Vietnam veteran Anse Caulfield in leading a team of former soldiers fighting poachers and rescuing exotic animals from captivity in private zoos and hunting ranches on the Georgia coast. To some degree, then, the novel departs from Brown's focus on the past to explore more contemporary worlds and issues, like those of "Rhino Girl." On the other hand, we can also sense an extension of several other interests Brown has explored in his published fiction. One is attention to the lives of veterans, at least one of whom has appeared in every book Brown has published, including Callum of *Fallen Land*, Lawton of *The River of Kings*, and Rory of *Gods of Howl Mountain*. Though Brown himself is not a veteran, he has explained this interest by way of both his father's and his own generational experience of, respectively, Vietnam and 9/11. Another thread running through Brown's prior fiction is an interest in ecological ethics, which takes on central importance in the latest novel. Perhaps most significantly, Brown has always shown an interest in writing strong women characters, most notably the co-protagonists Ava of *Fallen Land* and Granny May of *Gods of Howl Mountain*. Malaya of *Pride of Eden* is their bold successor.

Works Cited

Brown, Taylor. "Along the Little Amazon." *Salt Magazine*, December 30, 2016. http://www.salt magazinenc.com/along-the-little-amazon. Accessed November 16, 2018.

Brown, Taylor. *Fallen Land*. St. Martin's, 2015.

Brown, Taylor. "Georgia's Little Amazon." *Garden & Gun*, February–March 2018. https://garden
andgun.com/articles/georgias-little-amazon. Accessed November 16, 2018.

Brown, Taylor. *Gods of Howl Mountain*. St. Martin's, 2018.

Brown, Taylor. "How I Accidentally Wrote a Civil War Novel." Literary Hub, February 3, 2016.
https://lithub.com/how-i-accidentally-wrote-a-civil-war-novel. Accessed November 16,
2018.

Brown, Taylor. "Hurricane Florence: Diary of a Storm." *Garden & Gun*, September 18, 2018.
https://gardenandgun.com/articles/diary-of-a-storm. Accessed November 16, 2018.

Brown, Taylor. *In the Season of Blood & Gold*. Press 53, 2014.

Brown, Taylor. "The Lioness." *Sycamore Review* 27, no. 2 (Winter–Spring 2016).

Brown, Taylor. "Rhino Girl." *The Rumpus*, June 24, 2016. https://therumpus.net/2016/06
/rumpus-original-fiction-rhino-girl. Accessed November 16, 2018.

Brown, Taylor. *The River of Kings*. St. Martin's, 2017.

Brown, Taylor. "What I Saw When I Rode Out Florence." *New York Times*, September 18, 2018.
https://www.nytimes.com/2018/09/18/opinion/what-i-saw-when-i-rode-out-florence.html.
Accessed November 16, 2018.

David Joy is the author of the Edgar-nominated novel *Where All Light Tends to Go* (Putnam, 2015), as well as the novels *The Weight of This World* (Putnam, 2017), *The Line That Held Us* (Putnam, 2018), and *When These Mountains Burn* (Putnam, 2020). He is also the author of the memoir *Growing Gills: A Fly Fisherman's Journey* (Bright Mountain Books, 2011), which was a finalist for the Reed Environmental Writing Award and the Ragan Old North State Award. Joy has also received a fellowship from the North Carolina Arts Council. His short stories and essays have appeared in *Time*, the *New York Times Magazine*, *Garden & Gun*, and the *Bitter Southerner*. He lives in the mountains of southwestern North Carolina.

David Joy
Listening through the Violence

Rebecca Godwin

Born in 1983 in Charlotte, North Carolina, David Joy earned his undergraduate degree in literature and graduate degree in professional writing from Western Carolina University, where he met his mentor Ron Rash and studied with the creative nonfiction writer Deidre Elliott, as well as the novelist Pamela Duncan. In addition to these and other writers such as William Gay and Silas House, Joy credits his grandmother's Wilkes County Jack tales with inspiring his love of story ("An *Appalachian Heritage* Interview," 57). Staff writer for *Cashiers Crossroads Chronicle*, Joy writes fiction in the Appalachian noir tradition, a genre that he relates to work by Rash and Gay, as well as Cormac McCarthy, Flannery O'Connor, Harry Crews, Larry Brown, and William Faulkner—all influences for Joy's fiction. He sees "similarities between the grit lit that has come out of the South for so long and what has become popularized as noir." Stories in this category, sometimes called rural or country noir, Joy describes as "dark, often hopeless stories of working class people doing the best they can with the circumstances they are given" ("Country Discomfort"). His damaged characters, living with violence, trauma, misogyny, and drug addiction, seek redemption in their hardscrabble worlds, Faulkner's claim that "the past is never dead" confounding their fight against bloodline as well as social milieu.

Joy's first book, a memoir, sets up themes that his fiction explores. A finalist for the Reed Environmental Writing Award, *Growing Gills: A Fly Fisherman's Journey* (2011) examines youthful experiences that formed his love of the natural world, of quietness, of language. "We were a family of fishermen, the need for water pumping through each of our veins," he proclaims. "I never had a choice about this matter, and I'm glad for that" (25). Here Joy previews his fictional exploration of characters who seem destined by birth and others' decisions. His sense that "everything [he has] become . . . can be traced back to where [he] came from" (23) conveys that all is connected: past and present, people's fates, the natural world and the human. He channels Thoreau by going into the woods "to find places without people, without noise, without the frantic pace of modern society" (118). Taking readers through his college years, *Growing Gills* stands as Joy's philosophical edict. Quietly observing the environment while fishing and applying his considerable scientific knowledge, he decides to disagree with Nabokov's description of nature as deceptive. Joy sees nature's workings as "purely instinctual" and "humans [as] the only species who deliberately deceive" (73). This nature-human dichotomy plays out in his fiction, as does his fascination with evolution: as his characters respond to danger and pain, Joy tells with the brutal honesty he ascribes to nature the realistic truth that the struggle to survive can be ugly. His sense of the fish hierarchy—he never intentionally kills a trout, that "most well-dressed fish" whose beautiful coloration inspires his awe (39)—reflects his fiction's focus on human hierarchies, the social and economic inequalities that harden working-class characters whose despair erupts in cruelty. Reflecting on losing a battle with a native trout, Joy notes failure's value: "I seem to learn more about myself during my darkest hours than I ever do during the short-lived seconds of perfection" (181). This insight governs his fiction, where characters act out their darkest selves.

Like his other works, Joy's first novel is set in Jackson County, painting a bleak picture of Appalachian drug culture. A school dropout, narrator Jacob McNeely ponders the trappings of birth as *Where All Light Tends to Go* (2015) begins: "I'd let what I was born into control what I'd become. Mama snorted crystal, Daddy sold it to her, and I'd never had the balls to leave." His community, where kids "swiped prescription drugs from parents' medicine cabinets" and parents had "no clue of who their children had become" (3), offers few positives. Jacob's potential to move beyond his "lifetime of disappointment" (11) centers on a girl determined not to let her own family's inadequacies hold her back: Maggie, whom he has loved since childhood, "never let anything outside of herself decide what she would become." That Maggie sees in him "something worth saving" (54) helps him to escape his father's misogyny. But this gruesome tale's end finds Jacob continuing his family's violent legacy in an act of retribution that ironically seems to set things right in this off-kilter world.

Joy complicates this fast-moving story by telling it through the eyes of an eighteen-year-old bereft of proper adult guidance. Jacob's domineering father, Charlie McNeely, ensnares his son in an illicit drug business that he runs under cover of an auto repair shop, complete with money laundering and local policemen on his payroll. Ordered to ensure that an addict caught stealing from his own family to pay for his habit cannot identify his drug source, Jacob arrives to see the Cabe brothers, who have wired the addict in a chair, douse his cuts with sulfuric acid. After a revolting scene of screams and peeling skin, Jacob helps the brothers dump Robbie Douglass down an embankment. Jacob's nightmares prove his oft-mentioned unsuitability for such brutality, a trait his father calls weak. When Jacob mixes alcohol with Xanax to try to forget Robbie's "body wrapped crooked as hell around that rock" (40), his vomiting provokes his father's disgust: "Get the fuck up now, and be a goddamn man. . . . Quit being a fucking pussy about it and get up!" (41). In this scene, his father cares only that Jacob has beaten up a high school boy for urging Maggie to snort methamphetamine, or "crank": "Looks like there might be a little of that McNeely blood in you after all" (41). Jacob keeps his response to himself: "That's what I was scared of" (42).

This torturous father-son relationship drives the plot, setting up the question of whether "blood will tell," as the novel's epigraph from Cormac McCarthy's *Blood Meridian* suggests: "Only now is the child finally divested of all that he has been," it begins. Jacob mostly bends to his father's will. When a dog discovers Robbie, miraculously still living, Charlie McNeely shoots the Cabe brothers to prevent their exposing his role in the crime. Jacob drives the brothers' pickup truck, their bodies beside him, to a lake where his father, with keys to a barge, adds them to the watery graveyard holding his untold number of murder victims. Later, Jacob bolts when finding Robbie's mother in the hospital room where he plans to kill Robbie, her presence triggering his grief over his own wasted mother. Jacob stands up for his mother's humanity and sees the complexity of addiction: "I'd never blamed her for what she was" (140). He also knows that no woman, not his mother and especially not Maggie, deserves the attitude his father expresses about all females: "If they didn't have pussies, the dumpsters would be full of them" (45). After his mother's suicide with a gun her husband provides, Jacob demands a proper funeral and reflects on the cause-effect of human behavior when burying her ashes beside her parents and baby brother, killed in a lightning-strike house fire: "Even at a young age, I remember thinking that all that pain probably had something to do with how she turned out" (210). Daddy's raging wails after Mama's death make the son realize that this cruel father also has buried pain. But by the time Jacob overcomes his culture's model of taciturn masculinity and accepts Maggie's proposal that he go with her when she leaves for college, Joy throws another kink into Jacob's struggle to find a family and new identity.

The turns near the novel's end lead to clarity for Jacob. The one man who showed Jacob "what love felt like" (172), holding him after he finds his mama's body, deceives him. When Jacob reveals that his daddy leaves a Bible beside his victims' bodies, Lieutenant Rogers realizes that McNeely killed his brother years earlier. In reprisal, Rogers gruesomely murders McNeely and his girlfriend, after suggesting to Jacob that he get his money out of his daddy's safe before deputies arrive. But Rogers steals all but one wad of bills, and when officers appear before Jacob leaves, he texts Maggie the location of his money that she is to use for college tuition. He then calmly shoots Rogers. His act brings resolution: "I'd known I had it in me [to kill a man]. If there was one thing my father had given me, it was that. Killing Rogers would make things square, and if there was no getting out, then the best I could hope for was square" (256). Preparing to turn himself in, Jacob ponders his mother's staring at an Indian in a picture, "wondering where he was headed off to" (141). Jacob had mused at her funeral, "The closest I'd ever come to understanding an idea as big as God was the light that flickered in the eyes of the living. . . . There was a place where all light tends to go, and I reckon that was heaven. That lighted place was what that Indian had his eyes fixed on" (204). Owning his crime, Jacob travels "where that Indian had never had the courage to go": "I ventured out into that middle ground . . . and I finally understood that there'd never been any difference between here or there. Only the middle ground of this wicked world mattered . . . and those who were born with enough grit to brave it" (260). His own capacity for good and evil—helping Maggie get to a better life, killing Rogers for tricking him, bearing responsibility for his father's murder—is a moral ambiguity that Jacob accepts. Unable to stop "sinking down in [his] blood" (138), Jacob nonetheless brings his search for redemption to satisfying closure by meeting his fate with dignity.

Joy's second novel follows the first's themes, with the past creating a snare for young Appalachians again suffering the illegal drug culture's ruinous effects. *The Weight of This World* (2017), winner of the 2018 Tillie Olsen Award for Creative Writing from the Working Class Studies Association, begins with gut-wrenching horror: twelve-year-old Aiden McCall sees his father blow the top of his mother's head off and then shoot himself. In this unsettling prologue, Aiden predicts that he will become his father, for "blood always tells" (3). Aiden is placed in a group home so that he can establish a "normal" life, but he runs away, wandering into a hunting camp where failed men, "bad fathers," go to escape their responsibilities. When rescued by a likewise damaged adolescent male, Aiden begins a journey deeper into a "world turned sour" (2), a world that tests his desire to make something positive of his life.

Aiden's partner in despair is Thad Broom, doomed when born to a young girl raped by a church elder. Resenting the reminder of that painful experience, which leads to family and community rejection, April allows her abusive second husband to move teenage Thad into a run-down trailer, a makeshift abode that Thad opens up to young Aiden. The boys develop a brotherly relationship, fishing and surviving without parental guidance in a freedom reminiscent of Huck Finn's, with memories of "nights so still that as they paddled across the sky's reflection on Balsam Lake, the borrowed canoe seem[ed] to slice the moon in half" (12). After the World Trade Center attacks of 9/11, Thad enlists in the army and returns from Afghanistan with post-traumatic stress disorder as well as a ruptured disc. His panicked murder of a young Afghani girl, followed by a blast that kills a fellow American infantryman, helps to explain Thad's emotional instability:

> What haunted Thad was the realization that he lived in a place where both sides of good and evil saw that girl's death as an act of heroism. Evil men strapped explosives to a child's body in the name of God, and good men promoted Thad from private first class to specialist for pulling the trigger. In the end, she was just a girl and Billy Thompson was just a schoolteacher, and the two of them died together. Those were the only truths to be had. To think

either side was moral was a goddamn lie, and that was the biggest problem of all because Thad needed there to be a morality to it. (32)

Thad returns home to an equally senseless world: no mother who loves him, no father at all, "at least one person in every holler who cooked dope" (44). Out of work since the housing bubble burst, Thad and Aiden get money from crimes such as stripping abandoned houses of copper wiring. Addicted to crystal meth, Thad spends all his money on drugs or alcohol. Joy demonstrates the complexity of his unsavory characters in Thad's wish to "pray for forgiveness, pray that there was a God who could understand" (33). Yet the need for justice goes askew. When Doug Dietz, a drug addict and child molester, kills Thad's dog as payback for Thad's beating his addicted sister and her friend, drug-crazed Thad murders the girls before reenacting an Afghani retribution story, cutting the soles off Doug's feet before making him climb rocky hills to the place where he finally dies. As Thad blurs his current brutality with memories of war and suffering Afghani children, Joy's meaning seems clear: war's wickedness plays out again in the evil its haunted participants continue to perform.

Drug violence and past traumas shape characters' forward movement. After Thad and Aiden witness the accidental suicide of their stoned drug dealer, when a "thrash of blood, chunks like grayed hamburger, let loose across the room" (50), Aiden steals drugs to sell so that he can forge a new life. Tricked by a Mexican dealer recommended by a swindler childhood acquaintance, Aiden is badly cut and beaten. But thinking of a little Mexican girl and that swindler's boys softens Aiden's desire for revenge: shooting their father will "be setting up those two boys to be just like him." For the first time, he sees that "a man had choices" (250). Like Jacob McNeely, Aiden's final choice shows his father's blood, but also liberation. Aiden tortures April's church deacon rapist in the bad fathers' hunting camp and looks forward to killing him: "There'd be a glint of light in this wicked world because of something he'd done" (260). Punishing the one responsible for April's and Thad's suffering lightens "all the weight of this world" (218) when April starts a new life by accepting wealthy outsiders' low bid on her land. Aiden's revenge for others' pain moves him toward redemption more effectively than Thad's earlier confession to a preacher, whose promise of God's forgiveness fails to persuade Thad to "pay what [he owes] in this old world" (228). Thad shoots himself, ironically unaware that the deacon he threatens with his gun admits unfilled fatherly duties in his repeated "I'm sorry" (229).

The Line That Held Us (2018) moves away from the earlier novels' drug culture and profanity to focus more on class prejudice. When Dwayne Brewer, his family called "trash" all his life, sees a teenager in Walmart harass an impoverished boy, he makes the teen dunk his expensive shoes in a toilet, echoing O'Connor's "A Good Man Is Hard to Find" by thinking the teen "might've been all right if it had been a gun to his head every second of his life" (14). Dwayne's vengeful rage over his brother's accidental murder reflects an Old Testament "eye for an eye" justice, and his sensitivity to suffering triggers a biblically based fatalism, his meanness toward those who unintentionally shatter his life showing again a haunting moral complexity.

Like its precursors, this novel begins with an intensity that does not let up. Darl Moody shoots Carol Brewer, mistaking him for a boar as Carol pilfers ginseng from a neighbor's posted land where Darl likewise poaches deer. Knowing the Brewer reputation for callousness—that name rivals McNeely in Joy's first novel—Darl asks his best friend, Calvin Hooper, to help him bury the body. Suddenly these two hardworking buddies find themselves trapped. Darl hunts and fishes for his widowed mother and sister, whose husband makes little money after seizures result in a lost driver's license, and he wonders who will put food on their tables if he turns himself in. He decides to live with guilt to avoid hurting others. But when Dwayne Brewer sees images of Darl on the landowner's game camera and later finds Carol's pocketknife in Darl's truck bed, he tortures Darl until he identifies his accomplice. He then kills him. That Darl's basic goodness renders him incapable of shooting Dwayne when he had a chance deepens the moral ironies.

The lines that bind these characters—friendship, family, love, desperation, vengeance—place them on a ghastly journey. Calvin pays his own price for helping his friend. Dwayne forces him to dig Carol's body up and then leaves him unconscious in the dug-out grave. Lying to authorities whom he alerts to Darl's murder, Calvin realizes that "a man's mind is its own kind of hell" (112). When Dwayne kidnaps his girlfriend, Angie, almost killing her before locking her in a macabre cellar, ultimatums and ensuing events push Calvin toward Dwayne's predicament, facing how far he will go to save the one thing he loves more than himself. Dwayne wants others to learn the lesson that "deep down enough, every living thing [is] exactly the same" (182). Even Angie discovers her capacity to act to protect her unborn child.

Dwayne poses core theological questions as the grisly story unfolds. He carries his brother's corpse to their grandfather's cellar, washing it and wailing in guilt for not protecting his "too soft" baby brother (116). This place holds "memories of kin and the closest things he'd ever known to love" (95). Gnawed by rats and infested with flies, Carol's body literally falls apart when Dwayne tries to transport it to the beautiful wooded place their grandfather took them to as children. Dwayne reads scripture to Carol's corpse, seeing that, like Christ, he was "born at the bottom" (142). As children, he and Carol were ushered to a church's back pew because congregants saw them as trash. "Why He would fill a world with this kind of suffering" (144) has long puzzled Dwayne, who ultimately decides that God has "one sick, sick sense of humor" (170). Dwayne survives his suffering by bringing those who are "no better" than he to share it (227). To this miserable man, Joy assigns his own view that nature trumps humanity: "The only thing He ever got right . . . was these mountains," Dwayne avows. "These trees. These creeks" (170). When Dwayne tells Calvin that his clearing land for development is worse than what he has done, adding that Calvin thus has "spit in the face of God" (181–82), we hear Joy's roar against humanity's desecration of the land.

The Line That Held Us shares Joy's other works' focus on the connection of people and place. Describing the land that Calvin's ancestors settled before 1850, the narrator says, "Here there was blood tied to place the same as there were names tied to mountains and rivers" (34). No wonder native-born folks resent tourists and seasonal residents despite their providing income for working-class Appalachians. While Joy's dark stories take place in the place he knows, he recognizes the danger that readers will see his gritty fiction as perpetuating negative Appalachian stereotypes, particularly those of poverty, drug addiction, and violence. He argues that he means not to stereotype but to capture the human experience:

These are books about desperate people who have been backed into a corner and are left with no other option than to fight for their very survival. These are stories that, as Rick Bragg once put it, are "about living and dying and that fragile, shivering place in between." . . . That's a human story, one that could've just as easily been set in New York City. This is what Eudora Welty meant when she wrote, "One place understood helps us understand all places better." Violence and drugs are certainly present in Appalachia, just as violence and drugs are present in every place I've ever been. . . . These are stories about poverty and so if you want . . . to ask questions about what these books say about American culture, that's one place to start. (Joy, "One Place *mis*Understood")

In his essay "Digging in the Trash," Joy responds to a reviewer's suggestion that he "leave the peeling trailers, come down out of the hollers, and try writing about *people* for a change." For many, Joy understands, "trailer trash" does not equate to humanity. When he explains here that "violence is tied directly to . . . being heard," he shows the serious social value of his gripping, lyrical Appalachian noir.

Works Cited

Joy, David. "An *Appalachian Heritage* Interview: David Joy." Interview with Jason Howard. *Appalachian Heritage* 43, no. 1 (2015): 51–61.

Joy, David. "Country Discomfort: Author David Joy on Appalachian Noir and His Debut Novel." Interview with Daniel Ford. *Writer's Bone*, March 3, 2015. https://www.writersbone .com/interviewsarchive/2015/3/3/country-discomfort-author-david-joy-on-appalachian -noir-and-his-debut-novel. Accessed November 22, 2018.

Joy, David. "Digging in the Trash." *Bitter Southerner*, April 25, 2017. https://bittersoutherner .com/digging-in-the-trash-david-joy. Accessed November 22, 2018.

Joy, David. *Growing Gills: A Fly Fisherman's Journey*. Bright Mountain Books, 2011.

Joy, David. *The Line That Holds Us*. G. P. Putnam's Sons, 2018.

Joy, David. "One Place *mis*Understood." *Writer's Bone*, June 21, 2016. http://www.writersbone .com/featureslibrary/2016/6/21/one-place-misunderstood. Accessed November 22, 2018.

Joy, David. *The Weight of This World*. G. P. Putnam's Sons, 2017.

Joy, David. *Where All Light Tends to Go*. G. P. Putnam's Sons, 2015.

Lee Clay Johnson grew up around Nashville, Tennessee, in a family of bluegrass musicians. He holds a BA from Bennington College and an MFA from the University of Virginia. His work has appeared in the *Oxford American*, *The Common*, *Appalachian Heritage*, *Salamander*, *Mississippi Review*, and *Ploughshares*. His debut novel, *Nitro Mountain*, was published in 2016. He lives in St. Louis and Charlottesville, Virginia.

"Spirit Came Through"
Lee Clay Johnson

David Gates

There are probably a lot of things I still don't know about Lee Clay Johnson, my longtime friend and bandmate, and currently my colleague in the MFA program at St. Joseph's College in Brooklyn. He gave a short version of his life story in a 2013 *Oxford American* profile of the bluegrass musician Dave Evans: "I left my home in Tennessee when I was eighteen, toured the country with a rock band, followed a girl up north for college, and then returned south to Charlottesville, Virginia" (124). Let's fill that in a little. His parents, who still live outside Nashville, had a bluegrass band that played shows with legends such as Jimmy Martin—whom Lee's mother, a nurse, tended in his last illness. Before touring with the rock band, Lee had been booted out of high school; after the rock band, he got into the historically Black Tennessee State University as a white minority student, then transferred to Bennington College—for which I'd thank that "girl," if I knew her name.

That's where I first saw him, a tall undergraduate playing a jazz accompaniment on upright bass to a reading by the poet Major Jackson. A few teachers and students in Bennington's MFA program were putting together an informal band; I approached Lee and asked, naively, if he, by any chance, might have an interest in country music. And I still had no idea he was a writer, until he got into the University of Virginia's MFA program.

And then I still had no idea whether or not he could *write*, until I began to read him. So my music buddy and fellow country boy—chainsaw wizard, bourbon drinker, and dead shot with an air rifle—had the gift, and the taste and the commitment to go make use of it? Good to know. That Dave Evans profile, "Will You Carry On?", shows what an admirable nonfiction writer he is; so does his moving personal essay in 2016 for Literary Hub, "How to Write Deep in the Woods with a Dog by Your Side," about the genesis of his novel *Nitro Mountain* (and his drowning of an injured fawn), as does his perceptive introduction to "Lost Classic: The Poems of Breece D'J Pancake," published in 2012 in the journal *Appalachian Heritage*. For all I know, he's got a volume of his own poems up his sleeve.

But he has given most of his energy to fiction, and his first published story, "Palace" (2010), already suggests where he would be taking it in his 2016 debut novel, *Nitro Mountain*. "You can't just bring home a girl, promise her a warm room full of drugs, and not give it to her" (75), a down-and-out woman complains to that story's narrator. And there it is: degeneracy spiked with comedy. Or is it the other way around? Flannery O'Connor, one of his acknowledged influences, would have understood his work perfectly, and her 1960 essay "Some Aspects of the Grotesque in Southern Fiction" seems to fit *Nitro Mountain* as accurately as it does *Wise Blood*. The "grotesque" writer, O'Connor says, is

> looking for one image that will connect or combine or embody two points; one point in the concrete, and the other is a point not visible to the naked eye, but believed in by him firmly, just as real to him, really, as the one that everybody sees. It's not necessary to point out that the look of this fiction is going to be wild, that it is almost of necessity going to be violent and comic, because of the discrepancies that it seeks to combine. (42–43)

Nitro Mountain, set in the Appalachians of western Virginia, is rooted in the concrete, the minutely observed physical world, though the inhabitants of this still-beautiful landscape aren't much impressed with it. Johnson writes:

> "I'm staying. . . . Right at the top of that stupid mountain."
> "Which one?"
> "The stupid one." She pointed past the wall.
> "They're all stupid," I said. (59)

The mountain itself, ruined by a coal company, and the schematically juxtaposed towns, Ashland and Bordon, and their bars, the Hickory and its dark counterpart Durty Misty's, are all invented; but in Marianne Moore's phrase, there are real toads in these imaginary gardens. A touring band's van "reek[s] of body odor, cigarettes and spilled beer.... The passenger bucket seat was sprung and I could feel the wires under me" (42). A character's bottom teeth are "thin and burnt-looking like used matches" (55). A bartender has "orange cracker crumbs at the sides of his mouth. His hair [is] caught up in a bad Elvis situation. Paper clips [hold] some of it together" (7). A country lawyer's suit is "wrinkled in the back from sitting" (38). Yet these photorealistic visual and tactile details point to other realities. As Johnson wrote of Pancake's poetry, "Something about the writing existed beyond the words of the page. Spirit came through" (23). The sight of a single leaf in the wind leads a character to imagine "a small hole, a little puncture wound in the sky. What if there was an entire world behind the surface of this one? A darker place made of all the things we hide?" (77). And the language seems to suggest that the lawyer with the wrinkled suit is leading his DWI client to some higher court: "He showed me to a cheap pew, then went up and stood near the judge's throne" (38).

O'Connor's sense of a mystery behind the visible, of course, is specifically Christian (and more specifically Roman Catholic). Johnson's characters, southerners that they are, at least know the lingo. Here's the scary Arnett Atkins, he of the bad teeth, improvising a sermon as he's about to shoot his girlfriend (don't worry—just a flesh wound), and sounding much like O'Connor's Misfit in "A Good Man Is Hard to Find":

> The day He come to me, it was the most mysterious thing. Almost out of nowhere. Like back from the grave. Jesus come from a place you never been. Never seen before. Someplace you don't come back from. Not usually. That's what makes him Him. Your Jesus, He come back from the dead. For you. He rose from that grave with a sword. (121)

But this is just one of his drink-and-drug-addled riffs; Johnson's people are, literally, beyond belief. To the extent they have a credo, it might go something like this:

> Arnett knows you can't do over what you've already done. He knows that. And if you try to, that's you going back on yourself and still not fixing shit.

Like any of it could be fixed anyway. It's all fucked up and you can't unfuck it up, shouldn't even think about it. That's you putting everything that makes you who you are in the dump, and then what are you? Nothing. Absolutely fucking nothing left of you, except for the trouble you started, and then you can't even stand behind that and say, That's right, I done that. I stood up for myself. No, you got to have something to live by. Some people have religion, family—shit like that. You got you and what you done. (156)

This homegrown existentialism gives even the most degraded of Johnson's people—even Arnett, drug dealer, degenerate, and murderer—a bedrock dignity and integrity. As children, they were sexually abused, dumped in foster care, and hardly, let's say, exposed to the best role models: "Dad got pissed when he heard I'd found work and asked if I thought I was better than he was" (53). As adults, they drink, do drugs, cheat, and engage in only-sometimes-consensual sexual violence. On the way to his DWI appearance, the bass player Leon looks at Confederate statues in the town square and considers them "an encouragement to people like me: It's okay, we all lose eventually" (38). But they are not in love with being their own Lost Causes; that would be a decadent luxury. Leon goes on tour with a band even though he is wearing a cast on his broken arm. Jones Young, the country singer whose band Leon plays with, keeps performing and writing songs despite his almost certain failure to become a Nashville star, like his namesake George Jones. Larry, Jones's mentor and substitute father, lost two fingers and can no longer play guitar, but he runs a modest honky-tonk (whose real-life model may be Dave Evans's Bluegrass Palace in eastern Kentucky) to give local musicians a showcase: "Now that the coal's gone, music's our only damn export" (181). Jennifer, Arnett's frightfully abused girlfriend, gets away from him and makes a life for herself working at a pool hall across the border in Kingsport, Tennessee. (But did she really think he wouldn't find her?) The novel's last line suggests that Jennifer is pregnant with Arnett's child—a prospect appalling, I should think, to anyone but a committed pro-lifer. But Jennifer has a compulsion to live on the edge—"Maybe in normal society you're not worried every day. But when there's nothing wrong, what's the point?" (201)—and almost any form of human engagement is preferable to nullity. "You are not alone. I say it out loud" (208). And Arnett justifies his video voyeurism—perhaps the least of his crimes, though perhaps the most disgusting—as an embrace of our common humanity:

I put a camera in the toilet bowl. Maybe you've heard of me. Toilet Bowl Guy. . . . I'm not ashamed. It's all happening anyways, all that piss and shit. Why can't I watch . . . ? It's not like it's not happening if I can't see it. . . .

People ought to be open with each other. Share what's on the inside of ourselves, you know? I'm a caring person. I like to know how a woman feels on the inside. (70)

Sure, this is insane. But if Jennifer is the human heart of the novel, Arnett is the mad truth teller. As Johnson wrote in his Literary Hub essay, "When he showed up with all his demons, he pulled things together." Early in the novel, he confronts the bass player Leon, who has gotten a job bagging groceries in a food store:

"Who are you?" he said. "And why?"
    I didn't answer. . . .
    "Here's a better question. What do you want to be?"
    "That's deep," I said.
    "Answer the fucking question, hunch."
    Maybe he actually didn't recognize me. "I don't know," I said.
    "That's your problem. You need to make a decision." (55)

Maybe it's a coincidence, but Arnett is echoing a crucial moment in Johnson's nonfiction piece about Dave Evans. Evans, the genius banjo player and singer, has just finished up a song with some competent hobbyist musicians who have showed up at his Bluegrass Palace. "Y'all sounded fine," he tells them. "Y'all sounded fine, for what you're doing. But you ain't made the decision, see." This is the language of religious conversion, a call to an ultimate seriousness. Compare Alec Baldwin's monologue to the feckless salesmen in the film of David Mamet's *Glengarry Glen Ross*:

A-I-D-A. Attention, Interest, Decision, Action. Attention—do I have your attention? Interest—are you interested? I know you are, 'cause it's fuck or walk. You close or you hit the bricks. Decision—have you made your decision for Christ? And Action. A-I-D-A.

(And maybe *this* is a coincidence, but as a Bennington undergraduate working AV, Lee Johnson used to have to cue up this clip twice a year at the MFA students' orientation.)

Only the country singer Jones Young approaches Arnett's radical seriousness—Johnson artfully juxtaposes the two of them in the novel's long middle section—but Jones, however self-defeating, is ultimately sane, a citizen of this world, doggedly piecing his songs together. ("His songs seemed so simple," Leon reflects when he comes across some of Jones's manuscripts, "that I never thought of the time he put into them" [43]). Arnett is a creature from beyond. As Johnson wrote in his essay on writing the novel:

> I felt like I was watching him come into *being*. . . . Arnett was a blessing, a gift, flowing from the back of my head and out through the end of my pencil. He came so quickly, in a flash, that I remember sitting at my desk, around one or two in the morning, and watching the lead wear down beneath his weight.

This description suggests the fused discrepancies O'Connor had in mind: the "grotesque" writer—any writer, I suppose—is both Jones and Arnett. The one must sit down at a real desk, with a real pencil in hand, to summon the mystic, the terrifying other.

I don't mean to make too much of the point, but violent *and* comic, O'Connor said—and in Johnson's fiction, they're often inextricable. "Let me go get you some water," Arnett tells Jennifer. "I never shot a girl before" (121). Johnson has a Carver-like ear for poetically inarticulate speech—"Dude fucked with the wrong dude" (56), says the narrator of his 2018 story "Four Walls around Me to Hold My Life"—and especially for the vagaries of drunk or stoned talk, as in this dialogue from the same story: "'My brother was in the army,' I said. 'Or the military or the navy or whatever.' And we both lost it. 'Damn,' I said. 'That weed's working'" (60). In *Nitro Mountain* he gives Jennifer a line Denis Johnson might have been proud to have written: "We were transporting what he called Robot, a mixture of heroin and meth, and we felt good about the dynamics of the product" (196–97). And *Nitro*'s ex-cop, stripped of his badge and gun for using "necessary unnecessary force," who turns freelance lawman with a crossbow—is he a character out of Mayberry, or a Three Stooges farce? Johnson's comedy, like O'Connor's, ranges from the subtle to the outrageous—and can turn serious on a dime.

But maybe it's *always* serious. "Whenever I'm asked why Southern writers particularly have a penchant for writing about freaks," O'Connor wrote in her essay, "I say it is because we are still able to recognize one. . . . It is when the freak can be sensed as a figure for our essential displacement that he attains some depth in literature" (44–45). The reaction to Johnson's work seems strikingly like what O'Connor encountered so many years ago. When *Nitro Mountain* came out, he was asked to "write about writing a psychopath. A psychopath? Did they mean Arnett? I guess so. But I'd never thought of him as one. And if I had, I never could've written him" ("How to Write"). O'Connor's sense of "our essential displacement," predictably, is theological: the South, she believed, is "Christ-haunted," and the southerner is "very much afraid that he may have been formed in the image and likeness of God" (45). This is way too theological for Lee Johnson, I imagine, though the extent to which the South's residual Christianity might have shaped the deep structures of his own thought is one more thing I don't know. But there's a feeling in his work, and particularly in *Nitro Mountain*, of something gone awry, some displacement, some falling off from an ideal grace, beauty, humanity, and love; like O'Connor, he can spot a freak when he sees one. And in characters such as Larry, Jones, and above all Jennifer, who gets the last word, and even in the damaged and demonic Arnett, Johnson is able to recognize a spark of what he would probably hesitate to call the divine.

Works Cited

Glengarry Glen Ross. Directed by James Foley. Screenplay by David Mamet. With performances by Alec Baldwin, Jack Lemmon, Alan Arkin, Ed Harris, and Al Pacino. New Line Cinema, 1992.

Johnson, Lee Clay. "Four Walls around Me to Hold My Life." *Ploughshares*, Summer 2018, 54–65.

Johnson, Lee Clay. "How to Write Deep in the Woods with a Dog by Your Side." Literary Hub, May 16, 2016. https://lithub.com/how-to-write-deep-in-the-woods-with-a-dog-by-your -side. Accessed November 18, 2018.

Johnson, Lee Clay. Introduction to "Lost Classic: The Poems of Breece D'J Pancake." *Appalachian Heritage* 40, no. 3 (2012): 19–23.

Johnson, Lee Clay. *Nitro Mountain*. Knopf, 2016.

Johnson, Lee Clay. "Palace." *Mississippi Review* 38, nos. 1–2 (2010): 73–82.

Johnson, Lee Clay. "Will You Carry On?" *Oxford American* 82 (2013): 122–31.

O'Connor, Flannery. "Some Aspects of the Grotesque in Southern Fiction." In *Mystery and Manners*, edited by Sally and Robert Fitzgerald, 36–50. Farrar, Straus and Giroux, 1969.

Contributors

Destiny O. Birdsong is a poet, fiction writer, and essayist whose work has either appeared or is forthcoming in *African American Review*, *Best New Poets 2018*, *The BreakBeat Poets Volume 2: Black Girl Magic*, *The Cambridge Companion to Transnational American Literature*, *storySouth*, and elsewhere. She has received support from Cave Canem, Jack Jones Literary Arts, the Ragdale Foundation, MacDowell, and Tin House. She earned both her MFA and PhD from Vanderbilt University, where she currently works as a research coordinator.

Jean W. Cash is professor emerita of English at James Madison University. She had edited two previous collections of essays on southern writers and is the author of *Flannery O'Connor, a Life* and *Larry Brown, a Writer's Life*. Her most recent work has been on evocations of Nat Turner in fiction, poetry, and drama, published in 2020 in *Mississippi Quarterly*.

Kevin Catalano was born in Chittenango, a small village outside Syracuse, New York, which celebrates the birthplace of L. Frank Baum, author of the *Wizard of Oz* books. Kevin's debut novel, *Where the Sun Shines Out*, was published by Skyhorse Publishing in October 2017. His writing has appeared in *PANK*, *Fanzine*, *storySouth*, and *Gargoyle Magazine*, and his stories have been anthologized in *Surreal South '13*, *Exigencies*, and others. Kevin earned his MFA from Rutgers University, Newark, where he teaches.

Amanda Dean Freeman earned her MA from James Madison University; her current research focuses on the Rough South and issues of class in southern literature. She recently published an article on William Gay in *Southern Quarterly*.

David Gates is the author of the novels *Jernigan* and *Preston Falls* and two story collections, *The Wonders of the Invisible World* and *A Hand Reached Down to Guide Me*. He teaches at the University of Montana and in the Bennington Writing Seminars.

Richard Gaughran is associate professor of English at James Madison University in Harrisonburg, Virginia, where he teaches American literature and film studies. Recent publications include work on the Coen brothers, an article on contemporary films of the American South, and another on Don DeLillo's *The Names*.

Rebecca Godwin is professor of English at Barton College. She is the past chair of the North Carolina Writers Conference, past president of the North Carolina Literary and Historical Association, and past president of the Thomas Wolfe Society. She serves on the editorial boards of *North Carolina Literary Review* and the *Thomas Wolfe Review* and has published over a dozen book reviews, as well as twenty articles in scholarly journals or critical collections. A contributor to *Rough South, Rural South: Region and Class in Recent Southern Literature* (University Press of Mississippi, 2016), she wrote *Gender Dynamics in the Fiction of Lee Smith* (International Scholars Press, 1997) and is completing a book on Robert Morgan, focusing mainly on his fiction.

Joan Wylie Hall, a senior lecturer in English at the University of Mississippi, is the author of *Shirley Jackson: A Study of the Short Fiction* (Twayne, 1993). Editor of University Press of Mississippi's *Conversations with Audre Lorde* (2004) and *Conversations with Natasha Trethewey* (2013), she served as guest editor for *Southern Quarterly*'s special issue on Trethewey (Summer 2013). A book reviewer for several journals, she has published essays on Ruth McEnery Stuart, Eudora Welty, Tennessee Williams, Josephine Humphreys, Janisse Ray, Tom Franklin, and other southern writers.

Dixon Hearne, PhD, writes on the American South. His short fiction has been nominated for the PEN/Hemingway and PEN/Faulkner awards, as well as the Pushcart Prize. His novella won second place in the William Faulkner Literary Competition. Other work appears in *Oxford American, Louisiana Literature, Tulane Review, Post Road Magazine, The Southern Poetry Anthology, IV: Louisiana, Cream City Review, New Orleans Review, Big Muddy*, and elsewhere. He is working on new short story and poetry collections, as well as a novella.

Phillip Howerton is professor of English at Missouri State University–West Plains. His essays, reviews, and poems have appeared in numerous journals, such as *Arkansas Review, Big Muddy, Christian Science Monitor, Journal of Kentucky Studies, Midwest Quarterly, Plainsongs, Red Rock Review*, and *Slant*. He is the cofounder and coeditor of *Cave Region Review* and general editor of *Elder Mountain: A Journal of Ozarks Studies*. His poetry collection *The History of Tree Roots* was published by Golden Antelope Press in 2015, and his *The Literature of the Ozarks: An Anthology* was released by the University of Arkansas Press in February 2019.

Emily D. Langhorne is the associate director of the Reinventing America's Schools project at the Progressive Policy Institute in Washington, DC. She holds an MPhil in literatures of the Americas from Trinity College Dublin and an MEd from the George Washington University. She has taught high school English in Fairfax County, Virginia, and English as a second language in Santiago, Chile. Her writing has appeared in the *Washington Post, Forbes, The Hill, RealClearEducation, The 74, Washington Monthly*, and *Rough South, Rural South: Region and Class in Recent Southern Literature*.

Shawn E. Miller specializes in modern and contemporary American literature with an emphasis on the American South. His recent scholarly work has focused on contemporary writers of the Rough South. He teaches at Francis Marion University.

Melody Pritchard is a PhD candidate in English at the University of South Carolina, where she studies southern literature and rhetorical theory.

Nick Ripatrazone is the culture editor of *Image Journal*. He has written for *GQ, Rolling Stone, The Atlantic*, and the *Sewanee Review* and writes a monthly column on poetry for *The Millions*. In 2020 he published *Longing for an Absent God: Faith and Doubt in Great American Fiction*.

Bes Stark Spangler was professor emerita at William Peace University, where she was English Department coordinator and Alumna Distinguished Professor. While at Peace, she participated in an NEH American Studies Institute at Yale University. She earned her PhD from the University of North Carolina and published articles in a number of works, including *The Oxford Companion to Women's Writing in the United States*, *Dictionary of Literary Biography*, *Southern Writers: A New Biographical Dictionary*, and *Contemporary Southern Writers in Fiction, Poetry, and Drama*. She died in 2020.

Scott Hamilton Suter is professor of English at Bridgewater College, where he is also director of the Margaret Grattan Weaver Institute for Local History and Regional Culture and the American studies program. He has lectured widely and served as a consultant to a number of museums, including the Historical Society of Western Pennsylvania, the Museum of the Shenandoah Valley, and the Blue Ridge Institute. His publications include *Shenandoah Valley Folklife* (University Press of Mississippi, 1999), *Harrisonburg* (Arcadia Publishing, 2003), and *A Potter's Progress: Emanuel Suter and the Business of Craft* (University of Tennessee Press, 2020).

Melanie Benson Taylor is professor of Native American studies and house professor at North Park House at Dartmouth University. She is also editor of *Native South Journal*. She earned her BA from Smith College and MA and PhD from Boston University. She is the author of *Disturbing Calculations: The Economics of Identity in Postcolonial Southern Literature, 1912–2001* (2008) and *Reconstructing the Native South: American Indian Literature and the Lost Cause* (2012). Her "Capitalism, Consumption, and the Indian Imagery in Karen Russell's *Swamplandia!*" appears in *Navigating Souths: Transdisciplinary Explorations of a US Region* (2017).

Jay Varner is the author of the memoir *Nothing Left to Burn*. His work has appeared in *Bomb*, *Oxford American*, *Black Warrior Review*, and many other places. He teaches at James Madison University.

Scott D. Yarbrough is assistant vice president of academic affairs and professor of English at Charleston Southern University. He has published articles on Cormac McCarthy, Ernest Hemingway, and William Faulkner, among others; he is coauthor of *A Practical Introduction to Literary Study* and was the 2006–2008 Prose Fellow for the South Carolina Arts Commission. He was the 2017 president of the South Atlantic Modern Language Association and serves on the editorial board for the *Cormac McCarthy Journal.*

Photograph Credits

Index